Winning by Design

Frontispiece *'The Cardiff Wall' part of the display of models submitted in the first stage of the Cardiff Bay Opera House Trust competition, 1994. (Photograph: Steve Benbow.)*

'I am sure Mr Yarrow is a highly competent architect, but for something as important as new stands I propose we put an advertisement in a magazine read by architects, inviting any who are interested to send us plans and proposals in a competition so that we could study various possibilities and then make a choice.'

Conrad's consternation was matched by Yarrow's.

'But Marjorie –' Conrad began.

'It would be the normal course of activity, wouldn't it?' she asked with open eyed simplicity. 'I mean, one wouldn't buy even a chair without considering several for comfort and appearance and usefulness, would one?'

Taken from *Decider* by Dick Francis 1993
(Reproduced by permission of Michael Joseph Ltd.)

Winning by Design:
Architectural Competitions

Judith Strong

Butterworth Architecture
An imprint of Butterworth-Heinemann Ltd
Linacre House, Jordan Hill, Oxford OX2 8DP

   A member of the Reed Elsevier plc group

OXFORD   LONDON   BOSTON
MUNICH   NEW DELHI   SINGAPORE   SYDNEY
TOKYO   TORONTO   WELLINGTON

First published 1996

British Library Cataloguing in Publication Data
Strong, Judith
    Winning by Design: Architectural
    Competitions
    I. Title
    720.79

ISBN 0 7506 2493 0

Library of Congress Cataloguing in Publication Data
Strong, Judith.
    Winning by design: architectural competitions/Judith Strong.
    p.   cm.
    Includes index.
    ISBN 0 7506 2493 0
    1. Architecture—Competitions. I. Title.
    NA2335.S76   95–37491
    720'.79–dc20   CIP

Composition by Genesis Typesetting, Rochester, Kent
Printed and Bound in Great Britain by
Hartnolls Limited, Bodmin, Cornwall.

Contents

Acknowledgements

Winning by Design draws on the experience and expertise of many individuals and organisations.

People have given time to explaining details of practice and legislation, outlining policy directions and initiatives and debating the issues involved.

Architectural organisations, in this country and in Europe, have supplied background information, contacts and documentation.

Competition promoters and competition-winning architects have taken the trouble to complete questionnaires, discuss their projects and dig into their records to provide the details for the main text and the case studies.

This book is the product of their knowledge, patience and generosity.

The extract from *Decider* by Dick Francis (© Dick Francis 1993) is reproduced by permission of Michael Joseph Ltd.

1 An introduction to the debate

Architectural competitions make news. The new Opera House for Cardiff Bay, the British Museum Reading Room, the Tate's project for the Bankside Power Station have all helped to focus attention on this way of selecting an architect. They can also be controversial. The headline 'Nobody wins' captioned an article in *The Sunday Times* (October 1994) in which architectural correspondent, Hugh Pearman, savaged the competition system:

> Of all the self-serving nonsense that is regularly spouted about architecture, you can guarantee that one subject will provoke more claptrap than any other; competitions. They are the Achilles heel of Civic Architecture, are nearly always unsatisfactory either in their organisation or their outcome, waste a huge amount of people's time and money, and frequently result in winners that are never built or, if built, are bad, unpopular or sometimes both. Why do we bother with them?

A few weeks later, the same newspaper published another article (4 December 1994). Written by Richard Rogers and Mark Girouard, it was headlined 'Everybody wins' – the subject? Architectural competitions. Contrasting the British experience with that of other European countries, they write:

> France has developed a competition culture . . . the result has been dramatic. Some of the best buildings of the late 20th century have been built in France (not all by French architects): the Parisian grand projects are well known, but there are scores of excellent smaller-scale public buildings – schools, kindergartens, swimming pools, health centres – many built by young architects promoted by their universities and municipal authorities.

Starting points

Are competitions the 'Achilles heel' or do they represent a more enlightened approach to design which could lead to a better environment for us all? There are no simple answers. In deciding to write a book about the subject, I set out to analyse what has been happening over the past decade, to establish facts, explore issues and look for possible routes to be followed. My knowledge of the subject is based on the ten years I spent as Competitions Director at the Royal Institute of British Architects (1969–79), followed by six years as the Arts Council's Housing the Arts Officer. In researching this book, I talked to many people with an interest in the competition system: promoters, architects and designers, engineers and surveyors, lottery fund distributers, consultants and project managers, local authority councillors and staff, amenity and pressure groups, competition organisers in Europe, civil servants and administrators. Documents were collected, articles cut from the technical and national press, debates and discussions attended and questionnaires circulated to competition promoters and to winning design teams. This book sets out my findings.

It is written in response to a general feeling of unease about the value of competitions and uncertainty about how they should be organised. The aim is to throw light on the subject especially for those who are unfamiliar with the issues which fuel the debate. Much has changed in the last decade – particularly in what is now generally referred to as 'procurement' (i.e. the commissioning of goods or services). The competition system is one method of procuring design services and has to be considered in the context of this changing situation. But the debate about the value of competitions is not just about the more equitable distribution of design commissions (although this is seen as one important element). Those who argue for a wider use of the system do so for more ideological reasons relating to the need for openness in the distribution of public funds, for a better understanding of the design process, for public participation in the shaping of the built environment and for an overall improvement in the quality of what is built. Those who oppose any extension of the system may share these objectives. Their argument is that there are other ways of achieving them.

Myth or fact?

Which of the articles quoted above is telling the truth? Both of them are to a certain extent. Each writer can point to facts to support his case provided that he does so selectively. The overall picture is a more complicated one, as both these articles explain when they get down to details. Hugh Pearman almost concludes with the statement 'Competitions can undoubtedly produce good results' but then remembers his title and adds a final warning.

Richard Rogers and Mark Girouard concede that 'competitions can go wrong' but then point out that 'on looking around, it is painfully obvious that buildings commissioned without them can go even wronger'.

There are successful competitions. That is not in dispute. There are ones which 'go wrong' – although this is harder to define. Does a competition 'go wrong' if the winning design does not get built? There are all sorts of reasons why projects get abandoned, many of which are unrelated to the way the designer is selected. One competition promoter explained the position as follows: 'Whilst in principle the outcome appeared promising, unfortunately construction was overtaken by events as the office market deteriorated. I do not believe that one can say a competition is a success unless the building design is implemented and the economics tested.' For several years, the competition for the design of the Burrell Gallery in Glasgow was cited as an example of the failure of the system because the available funding was insufficient for the project to proceed. Inflation had eaten into the original endowment. When funding was finally secured the scheme went ahead as originally planned. The completed building won critical aclaim and the competition was agreed to be a success – same competition, same architect, same design.

Does a competition 'go wrong' if the result is controversial? This too is debatable. Architectural historians can point to many examples of buildings which were badly received when built but came to be appreciated by later generations (including some which were the result of competitions). This does not prove that all rejected competition-winning buildings would have been loved if built but it does show that 'controversy' is not a reliable measure of quality (or lack of it) when considered in the longer term.

Most people would agree that a competition has gone wrong if the winning scheme, having been selected by the assessors in accordance with the published conditions, is rejected by the promoting body. There are examples of this happening and it does so often enough to be a cause of concern. When the winning scheme is rejected in this way, it can leave a legacy of bitterness and distrust affecting competitors, assessors and the promoter. The reasons for this happening are diverse and the situation cannot always be avoided. But questions relating to the quality of preparation, the adequacy of consultation procedures, the constitution of the jury and the basis on which the selection of the winner was made, all need to be examined, as does the original motivation for the competition and the level of commitment involved.

Looking for evidence

What evidence is there to support the statements which continually recur when competitions are being discussed? The following quotations have all appeared in recent articles about competitions.

Competitions produce better buildings
No detailed research has been carried out, as far as I am aware, to prove this statement either way. Nobody would claim that every competition guarantees an award-winning building. It is more a question of probability and of creating a climate in which design issues are important. What can be demonstrated is that many of the architects who are regarded as the most gifted in design terms, have built their reputations in part through the competition system either in the UK or abroad.

Competitions saddle the promoter with young and inexperienced design teams
Only a small proportion of competitions represent the first commission for the winning architects. Promoters who fear such an outcome can use one of the pre-selection procedures or interview shortlisted competitors before they go through to the second stage. Even where a new practice is set up to carry through a competition winning design, the architects will not necessarily be inexperienced – or young. They will often have been employed in established practices and have taken responsibility for major projects. The winning architect does not work alone. Engineers, quantity surveyors and other specialist consultants all make up the design team. Young architects who enter competitions almost invariably do so in association with established consultants – it is one of the ways consultants build up links for future contracts.

In one recent competition, a surprising number of the first-stage winners turned out to be younger than is usual. Asked to comment the promoter said, 'We found this particularly appealing as it was obvious we were being given new ideas and not just a collection of bits which had worked elsewhere. It meant we could go back to basics and work things through with an architect who did not have a pre-conceived approach.' After the first-stage selection had been made, the promoter interviewed the short-listed competitors to check on both their capability to see the project through and their compatibility with key members of the project team. All six teams then went through to the second stage.

The statement quoted above could be turned on its head. Some promoters resort to a competition to avoid being saddled with an older architect who has been churning out the same 'tried and tested' solutions for far too long. This may not often be the stated reason for promoting a competition, but there is sufficient anecdotal evidence to suggest that it can be an underlying motivation.

The competition-winning projects which have been designed and built by young or newly-established practices have a very good record, both historically and in recent years. Several of the case studies in the second half of this book focus on projects where there were younger winners. Such projects do appear to require a greater input from the client – all the winning architects gave credit to the help and support they received – but this can be more than matched by the enthusiasm of the winning teams and their determination to 'get it right'.

Competitions cause controversy
Put in the words 'can occasionally' and the statement becomes irrefutable. Anybody who doubts it has only to look at the media coverage following the announcement of the result of the Cardiff Bay Opera House competition (1994–95). Controversy on this scale stays in the public mind. People still refer to the problems of the National Gallery competition and to the 'disastrous' Sydney Opera House competition, though the latter was held several decades ago.

When cited as a reason against promoting a competition, the controversy argument is not so clear cut. Is it the competition or the project itself which leads to trouble? When a competition results in a heated debate, it often raises issues which were inherent in the project from the outset. In an article 'Competitions: who really wins?' (*The Independent*, 25 May 1994), Arts Consultant, Adrian Ellis writes:

> Before a competition is set in train, the client really must ensure that the general proposal – be it an opera house, a museum or a stadium – has been debated. If not, then no matter how good the designs generated by the competition, they will be attacked in order to criticise the basis of the project itself.

High-profile buildings generate interest and this is heightened by the spotlight of a major architectural competition. (It is one of the reasons for holding a competition in the first place and can help the project get off the ground.) Occasionally, this spotlight focusses attention on criticism either of the way the competition was run or of the winning entry. When this happens it can test the promoter's commitment to proceed with the project. If the commitment is seen to waiver, the opposition rallies its forces and turns criticism into an all out attack.

Competitions consume an inordinate amount of time, money and energy
Competitions, particularly large scale open competitions, are costly to both the promoter and the architects who enter. Most of the cost is accounted for in terms of time spent – by the promoter in developing and preparing the brief and by the architects in analysing the problem and preparing design solutions. As far as the promoter is concerned, not all of these costs are add-on costs attributable solely to the competition. Additional time has to be spent and expertise brought in to secure a high quality product whatever design selection procedure is used.

Most of the time, money and energy spent on competitions is put in by the architects who enter. For the individual practice, the cost of preparing an entry for a major international competition could be as much as £100 000.

(This would be the top of the market figure for an international competition.) Multiply this by the number of entries and the cost to the profession has to be described as 'inordinate'. Though most competitions would not require an input of this scale, even the most committed competition supporters acknowledge the design cost problem. Their solution is to limit the amount of design work required in a competition to the minimum necessary for assessment to be made. Careful staging can also reduce the overall design input. More important, in their view, is that the effort is not wasted. They see no case for holding design competitions where projects are tenuous or where there is insufficient money to fulfil the commitments entered into.

Competitions can foist an architect on an unwilling promoter
Where this happens, something has gone wrong long before the result of the competition is announced. The system of an independent all-architect jury whose decision was final and binding was abandoned some thirty years ago. Juries can now bring in a range of interests and the promoter often selects both the chair and the majority. Promoters can also take advantage of a variety of other opportunities for closer involvement in the selection process. The professional institutes offer the promoter a range of options which have been shown to produce good results, but they have no monopoly on competitions. Those who consider their procedures to be too restrictive can approach other agencies or run their own competitions, provided they have the necessary expertise.

The competition system comes between the architect and the client
There is an issue which lies at the heart of the competition debate. It focusses on the process which architects regard as crucial to their work, the dialogue between the architect and the client. This dialogue (a mixture of question and answer, discussion, assessment, interrogation and analysis) is the process by which designs are developed. Where it starts, whether it can be split into sections, how important it really is and whether it exists at all in certain situations are all the subject of intense discussion. Many architects maintain that it underlies the whole relationship between architect and client. They regard it as the key factor in the successful transition from concept to design and from design to implementation.

How does this affect competitions? The traditional design competition system aims to provide a set of rules which ensure that everybody who takes part does so on an equal basis. Anonymity is retained throughout. No contact is permitted between the competitors and the promoter, assessors and advisers other than in specified written form until the final selection has been made. The brief is issued, designs submitted and a decision reached. The result? Scrupulous fairness but no dialogue. The promoter cannot discuss hopes and expectations, no hints can be given as to what would be acceptable and what would be offputting, competitors cannot probe, alternatives cannot be explored, questions tend to be factual if not banal as no competitor wants to reveal his or her line of thinking. Ideas have to be put across in written or visual form. If they are obscure or even completely misunderstood there is no opportunity to talk this through. Decisions have to be made and hunches backed without recourse to the dialogue.

In some situations this freedom to develop ideas can be creative and many people would argue the case for retaining this type of competition as one option. Others find themselves restricted and feel they cannot work effectively within its procedures. Various innovations have been made over the years to enable some form of dialogue to take place – introductory seminars, informal question and answer sessions, individual briefing at the second stage, interviews and presentations. The problem is that once issues other than 'quality of design' begin to be introduced, anonymity is lost and the credibility of the system can begin to be undermined. For this reason the official international and European systems follow the traditional format very closely. The UK professional institutes have aimed to strike a balance between the desire for dialogue and the need to retain fair and equitable procedures and have introduced more flexibility into their systems. There is some pressure for them to go further.

The competitions system in a terminal muddle
The muddle is unlikely to prove to be a terminal one but it certainly exists. Over the past decade, many traditional practices have been discarded without anything new being put in their place. Previously-accepted principles no longer apply and definitions have become blurred and often unworkable. Architectural competitions used to be defined and regulated solely by the various professional institutes. Although these organisations still operate competition systems (and will manage projects for individual promoters) their competitions form only a part of the total number. A whole range of competitive selection procedures has been introduced, all referred to as 'competitions' by the media. At present, these are unco-ordinated and unregulated. No distinction is made between the good, the bad and the indifferent. When things go wrong, the adverse criticism which ensues is directed at the competition system, regardless of the fact that many of its principles and procedures may well have been ignored.

The issues outlined above are explored in greater detail in later sections of this book.

The relevance of the current competition debate

There are two events which have stirred up interest in the competition system. One is the introduction of the open market within the European

Union and the other is the launch of the National Lottery in the UK. Both these made their initial impact in 1994 but their influence will be long-term. Many of the implications for the competition system have still to be sorted out.

European legislation now covers the processes by which architects and other members of the design team are commissioned. (Information on how this operates and who is affected by it is given in Chapter 9.) In essence, it places competition, in some form, at the centre of the commissioning process. The legislation also spells out how 'design contests' shall be run.

The UK national lottery promises to inject considerable funding into capital projects. Questions of how the money is to be distributed have been high on the agenda and, right at the outset, a commitment was made to establish 'quality of design' as one of the key funding criteria. The need for public consultation and the fair distribution of public money is also regarded as important. A debate on the subject of 'architectural competitions' was held on the BBC's *Late Show* soon after the lottery was announced. Rory Coonan, Director of Architecture at the Arts Council of England, made his position clear: 'The lottery will generate more competitions and this will be a good thing. Where public money is being spent, we are entitled to see, as tax payers, that as many people as possible get an opportunity' (Chapter 9 outlines the UK national lottery procedures).

There is a third area which could, in time, influence how architectural competitions are run and used. It relates to the way architects and design teams are selected. Both government and the construction industry (clients and service providers) are showing an increased concern about the quality of what is being built and are looking at ways of improving the current situation.

Competitions as a system of procurement

In a symposium to launch the competition for the New Museum of Scotland (see page 131), John Spencely, then President of the Royal Incorporation of Architects in Scotland (RIAS), was asked to speak on the subject of 'Why hold a competition?' He began by outlining the different methods of selecting an architect or design:

> You can do this by interview, that is the normal way. A few people sit round the table and compile a list of those they think might be suitable, or they go and look at their buildings, they take references from previous clients, and they make a decision. Or you can simply open the *Scottish Architects Directory* or *Yellow Pages* and pick one with a pin. You can ask your neighbour whom you should use: this is not uncommon. It is quite startling how many projects are achieved, or the selection of an architect is achieved, in that way. You can follow President

Mitterand, who simply decides on the basis of having visited a building that its architect shall be apppointed – a very simple way of doing it. There is a fee-bidding way where you ignore the potential quality of the product and simply go on price. There is nomination by a third party; you go to somebody else and ask them to choose an architect for you. And then there is nepotism. So those are all well-tried and well-tested ways of securing an architect.

This is an intentionally lighthearted approach to the rather heavy subject of procurement but it does give quite a comprehensive summary of the choices available. It also sets the decision to promote a competition in context. It is one procedure within a whole range of other options.

The debate about competitions tends to focus on whether the architectural competition is a better way of selecting an architect than through consideration of previous work and established experience. Trying to demonstrate that one system is preferable to another, whatever the circumstances, is unconstructive. Very few proponents of the competition system would recommend its universal application. They see it as an important but complementary part of a much broader quality-based procurement pattern. James Laidlaw, current President of the RIAS, writes in a letter to *Building Design* (February 1985), 'Those aspiring to quality should appreciate that design competitions are but one of a number of ways of achieving that – and that all methods have their strengths and weaknesses.'

There is, however, another reason for regarding the competition/direct appointment debate as not only unconstructive but as focussing on the wrong issues. Over the last decade, the system of direct commissioning has increasingly been replaced by one which requires an input of unpaid and unregulated competitive design work. How this came about and the effect it is having on practice in this country in general and competitions in particular is explored in Chapters 2 and 3.

2 The impact of 1980s' policies and legislation

The competition system goes back a very long way. Architectural historians have found references to a competition for the design of a building on the Acropolis in 448 BC, and its use is documented during the Renaissance period. The system has been revised and developed throughout this century and was reappraised and redocumented in a joint initiative by the Royal Institute of British Architects (RIBA) and the Department of the Environment (DoE) as recently as 1986. Similar procedures are used throughout the world, drawn up by professional institutions and governments in the individual countries or organised on an international basis by the International Union of Architects (IUA), working in association with UNESCO. Seen in this context, some may question why any problems relating to the use of the system have not, by now, been fully resolved.

Architectural competitions have to work within prevailing conditions. Their organisation is affected by and needs to respond to changes in the way the construction industry functions and in architectural practice. Just because a system was seen to work in some place at some time it does not mean that it will be equally effective elsewhere.

The responsibility for the development of the competition system in this country lay, for the most part, with architects and the institutions which they formed. For much of this century, the term 'architectural competition' could be regarded as synonymous with the competition formats defined by the professional institutes. An appreciation of how this came about and what has happened since, is crucial if the debate on the role which competitions now play in the procurement process is to be understood.

Reference is made throughout this section to the RIBA. It is not the only professional organisation involved in competitions. For some time, the RIAS (Royal Incorporation of Architects in Scotland) has administered its own system and, with the advent of the four distinct national lottery distributory bodies for arts and sports funding, it is likely that the Society of Architects in Wales and the Royal Society of Ulster Architects will develop as individual competition agencies. The Royal Town Planning Institute and the Institute of Landscape Architects also organise competitions. Historically the RIBA was responsible for developing the system in this country.

A brief and recent history

Although there are examples of the competition system being used throughout the centuries, the period of greatest impact in the UK was the nineteenth century. More than 2500 competitions were held between 1850 and 1900 alone producing numerous prestigious buildings and an archive of drawings for later historians. The system thrived but it did so in an atmosphere of controversy and scandal.

The system at that time was completely unregulated and this gave rise to a whole host of problems and complaints. Accusations were made of bias, of promoters being unduly influenced by presentation, of general incompetence and of widespread corruption. There are stories of promoters trying to put together parts of entirely separate projects (e.g. the top of this one and the bottom of that); of well-known architects sub-contracting work and presenting it as their own; and of the competition result being set aside by a professional assessor so that he could be appointed to do the job.

In 1880 a petition was drawn up comprising signed statements by 1340 architects, including Fellows and Associates of the RIBA and non-members, asking RIBA Council to devise a remedy for the unsatisfactory state of architectural competitions in the form of a scheme whereby all members of the profession could agree not to take part in any public competition unless a professional adjudicator of established reputation was appointed (Architectural Competitions Memorial, 1880).

Eventually the regulators got their way, initially in the form of recommendations covering qualified assessment, a reasonable prize fund, and a commitment to the winner on the part of the promoter. These became mandatory in 1907. Building on its success, the RIBA went on to strengthen the regulations, eventually introducing conditions which safeguarded the architect to such an extent that they almost killed off the competition system in this country. The promoter was required to appoint an all-architect jury, nominated by the president of the RIBA, and build the design the jury selected (or pay the designer of the winning scheme 1.5% of the estimated cost of building the project in compensation). After several decades of this regime had reduced the number of competitions to a mere trickle, the system was gradually modified and made more responsive to clients' requirements. Provision was made for the promoter to be represented on the jury and an element of choice was brought into the final selection.

Fee scales and regulated practice

For many years, architects worked to a fee scale (drawn up by the RIBA). It spelt out how much they would charge for any particular work (based on the design stage reached and taking into account the complexity and cost of the project) and what level of service the client could expect in return. The RIBA Code of Professional Conduct included a clause to the effect that 'no member may compete with another architect by means of a reduction of fees or by means of other inducements'. This meant that any design work commissioned from an RIBA member automatically incurred a set fee. If a client wished to commission several designs she or he was required to inform all the RIBA members involved and pay each of them the appropriate amount. The only other way a promoter could consider more than one design approach was to promote an RIBA-approved competition. Throughout this period, the vast majority of architects were members of the RIBA. (It was accepted procedure for public offices and for most practices to require that architects on their staff joined the RIBA.) This enabled the RIBA to maintain effective control of all forms of competitive work and the term 'architectural competition' became synonymous with 'RIBA-regulated competition'. (The IUA was recognised as having jurisdiction over any competition involving architects from two or more countries and the RIAS organised competitions along similar lines in Scotland.)

The impact of competitiveness

Throughout the 1980s, competitiveness was encouraged by a government committed to the concept of a market-led economy. The fee scales and codes which the professional institutes saw as regulating practice in the interests of both the architect and the client, were regarded as by the government as 'protectionist'. In 1977, the mandatory fee scale to which all RIBA members worked was declared unacceptable by the Monopolies and Mergers Commission (MMC). For some time after, RIBA members worked to a 'recommended fee scale' published in the book of terms and conditions, *RIBA Architects Appointment*, but in response to continuing pressure from the MMC and the Office of Fair Trading (OFT), the RIBA finally abandoned even the recommended scale (1992). An attempt was made towards the end of 1994, to reintroduce a fee guidance document but this move was immediately questioned by the OFT who considered it 'likely to restrict, to some extent, the degree of fee competition among RIBA members'. The issue is still a live one and the moves and countermoves of the various participants are likely to continue.

The abandonment of the first mandatory and then the recommended fee scales knocked away one of the main supporting structures in the RIBA's jurisdiction over competitions and effectively marked the end of any monopoly the RIBA had. Though the clause 'a member shall not enter any architectural competition which the RIBA has declared to be unacceptable' remains in the Code of Professional Conduct (rule 3.7), virtually no attempts have been made to enforce it. The alternating booms and recessions of the 1980s and 1990s weakened the RIBA's position and reduced its membership (both in actual numbers and as a proportion of the qualified architects in the country). During boom times practices took on architectural staff without worrying whether or not they became members of the Institute. During recessionary periods, the need to maintain a continuing flow of new commissions took precedence over adherence to the rules controlling competition.

Competitive work became the norm. The recession of the early 1990s arguably marked the low point of the profession's bargaining position. Clients with attractive commissions to offer were able to demand and get a great deal of design work from a number of different architects, much of it provided free of charge. Some observers claim that the profession's tradition of architectural competitions merely served to aggravate the position. Architect, David Rock, writes in the introduction to a report on a competition which he assessed:

> . . . the principle and marketing of the RIBA competition system has 'sold the pass' to the industry in spreading the accepted wisdom that architects (supported by the other professions) will work for free if it is called a competition.

The privatisation of services

As well as pursuing policies of deregulation in support of its market economy philosophy, the Thatcher government also pressed forward with measures to privatise public services. One of the results was that in-house teams of architects and technical advisers were disbanded. The existing staff were either made redundant or were relocated to less-specialised administrative groupings. As part of this policy, large commissioning organisations (e.g. both in the health and education services) were divided into smaller units, each responsible for its own affairs. Specialist areas of expertise were to be bought-in from private agencies rather than built up within the individual organisations.

During such a major process of re-organisation and redistribution of responsibilities it was inevitable that much of the professional experience which had been accumulated within these large organisations was dispersed or lost. The smaller units which replaced them had neither the need nor the resources to rebuild the expertise. The result was that many new client bodies came into existence which had no experience of buying into the construction industry and no established sources of advice. They applied the market criteria which were current in other areas. The practice of commissioning on the basis of 'lowest price for the job' became more widespread and 'tenders' were frequently invited for design 'contracts'.

This process of re-organisation was matched by a growth in the number and range of organisations and individuals offering advisory services. Their experience, expertise and the criteria by which they operated varied. Some sought to secure for their clients the best quality available in design and building terms; some interpreted 'best' in terms of some concept of value for money (seen either in the short or long term); and some considered that their clients were well served by negotiating for the cheapest price and service available (regardless of any quality implications). It was readily apparent that each of these aims could be furthered by holding some form of competition.

The different types of competition which are now being used are described in Chapter 3.

The profession's response

The professional institutes are funded by their members. Many of them are now facing difficult times financially and find that their capacity to respond to anything other than the immediate concerns of their members is limited. This is affecting the RIBA Competitions Service which has already undergone a 'value of money' scrutiny. It is expected to earn its keep from both its advisory and management services.

Once it lost its old monopoly position, the RIBA was left with a system but no authority to impose that system on others. The result was that many would-be competition promoters got hold of the documentation, took the system and adapted it for their own use. Competitions were being promoted which looked like RIBA competitions but did not necessarily follow their procedures or offer their safeguards. While seeking to fund its service through charging promoters prepared to work within its recommended procedures, the RIBA was providing its expertise for free (through the readily available documentation) to those who were effectively under-mining its authority and in some cases exploiting its members. Early in 1994, the RIBA took the decision to withdraw its competition documents from general circulation. Those who wished to use the carefully worked out procedures would have to pay. While its 'agency' role justified this course of action, it meant that only those who chose to appoint the RIBA as managers or pay for its advice and 'seal of approval', would be given guidance as to what constituted good competition practice. The RIAS, on the hand, seems to have been better able to maintain its influence on competitions and to balance the two roles. It has the advantage of working in a smaller and more integrated professional community but has also demonstrated a greater commitment to encouraging promoters to seek its advice and use its system.

Spurred into action by the increasing number of complaints about badly organised competitions and by the Arts Council's stated intent to encourage greater use of the competition system in its distribution of lottery funding, the RIBA finally began to address itself to the issue.

A consultative report published in the *RIBA Journal* (February 1995) set out the initial agenda. It outlines a three point plan 'with the aim of dragging up the standard of design competitions in the UK, getting the RIBA involved in more of this very fragmented market and ensuring that architects are properly remunerated'. Its proposals include providing a more integrated advisory service spanning all commissioning processes including competitions; upping the cost of RIBA competition services (consultancy, management and assessment) and introducing the 'competitive interview' into the RIBA competition system.

Construction industry concerns

Architects and the design teams with which they work are part of the much larger construction industry. By the beginning of the 1990s, problems related to the widespread application of market-led ethics and procedures were becoming apparent throughout the industry. Many of the problems related to the operation of the 'lowest cost tendering' method as applied to both building and design contracts. In July 1993, Sir Michael Latham was commissioned by the government to undertake a review of procurement and commissioning arrangements in the UK construction industry. The review was jointly funded by the Department of the Environment and a consortium of construction industry groups. The objective was to identify quality–price mechanisms for use throughout the construction process which would reduce conflict and litigation and encourage the industry's productivity and competitiveness. By the end of 1994, the initial report had been published and a Review Implementation Forum created, made up of representatives of the Construction Industry Council, the Construction Industry Employers Council, the Construction Liaison group, government and client bodies. The recommendations which are most likely to have an effect on the way design services are procured relate to:

- the preparation of a client's guide to briefing;
- a Construction Code of Practice covering project and contract strategy, project management, the selection of consultants and tendering procedures;
- a register of consultants.

These initiatives demonstrate a widespread interest in low-risk rather than in low-cost methods of procurement and in procedures which provide quality of both service and product. Selection systems which require the lowest tender are being replaced by some form of value for money assessment. While this may reduce some of the pressure on the design professions to cut their fees to the minimum in order to get a commission, it could also lead to an increased demand for competitive design work.

Quality of design

One of the lead organisations in pushing for more emphasis to be placed on design quality in public commissions is the Arts Council (formerly of Great Britain and now of England). Its Architecture Unit was set up in 1991 with the aim of promoting public education in architecture. The Unit's influence stems from the high profile of the Council itself and from the calibre of its Architecture Advisory Committee.

In 1993, the Architecture Unit commissioned a report from Prospect Research which examined the Government's design record and challenged it to back its commitment to architectural patronage (*Architecture and the Executive Agencies*, published by the Arts Council, December 1993). The report looked specifically at the executive agencies, the recently hived-off civil service groups, which it identified as being 'at the vanguard of the new independent public sector'. The survey found that despite governmental rhetoric to the contrary, the message being passed down to the civil servants who procure buildings was that good design was a luxury they could not afford.

The Arts Council intended the report to stimulate debate. It saw the executive agencies as setting the pace for the whole of the public sector. 'Their attitude, experience and practice will have far-reaching effects on the next generation of public buildings.'

Government initiatives

The government also appears to be seeking a lead position in the 'drive for quality'. The initiative has been picked up by Environment Secretary, John Gummer in what has been termed his 'crusade' to lift the quality of town and country planning.

A consultative document, 'Quality in Town and Country', was issued and a nationwide series of conferences planned. The opening paragraphs of the consultative document set out John Gummer's credo. He writes:

As we secure economic growth and development we expect to enjoy our greater wealth through an improved quality of life. This means improving our surroundings; conserving and enhancing the environment of town and country. . . . Good urban design can reinforce a sense of community, whereas anonymous grey and alienating surroundings isolate the individual. A depressing environment destroys local pride, attracts crime, deters investment and leaves people feeling powerless. Yet quality attracts quality, good design attracts life and investment . . . if we improve our buildings and the streets and spaces which they define, we surely improve the quality of all our lives.

Both the reappraisal of 'lowest cost' procurement methods and the new quest for quality have implications for the competition system in that they influence the climate in which competitions operate. Where 'lowest cost' is the criteria both for selecting the design team and for securing the product (the building), clients will use competitions directed towards this end. Such competitions inevitably distort a system which was designed to serve a different set of objectives, and in the process turn professional opinion against their use. This has been the pattern over much of the last decade. If 'best quality' were to become the objective, the architectural competition system could have a more genuine and constructive role to play.

3 Competition and competitions

There are many forms of procurement in which two or more architects are required to submit designs in competition with each other in order to secure a commission. Many of the procedures outlined in this chapter could be described as a form of competition and most of them would be referred to as such by the press and media. This is one of the problems. The procedures are not all architectural competitions and would not be recommended by those calling for a more extensive use of the competition system. Some of them are not even regarded as a satisfactory way of selecting either an architect or a design for a building project.

The problems relating to the procurement of design services are wide ranging. It is the subject of a number of detailed expert studies and the process is currently being reviewed at many levels – by government, within the construction industry, through client consortia, by the professional institutes and in university departments. What follows is inevitably a simplification, in fact an over-simplification, of the issues. They are considered here only in so far as they have a direct impact on the effective operation of the architectural competition system in this country.

The different categories of competition identified in this chapter do not have any official status. The terms used to define them are a mixture of observed usage and invention (in order to clarify perceived distinctions).

Many commissions now fall within the jurisdiction of the EC directives and some of the procedures described below would not be applicable to projects covered by their rules (see Chapter 9).

Procedural roots

The procedures currently being used in the procurement of architectural and design services have their roots in three distinct systems of selection, traditional to the construction industry and to the design professions. These are: tendering for work; the 'selective search' to identify a suitable architect/ design team; and the architectural competition.

The tender

Bidding to secure a building contract is a long established and accepted procedure. It works as follows. The design team develop the design to the stage of detailed working drawings. Bills of quantity are then drawn up to establish the cost of materials required for construction. Competitive bids are invited from selected building contractors who work out their costs based on the information supplied and put in tenders for the project. The client appoints the contractor who offers the best deal. This system is widely used for the commissioning of works (i.e. buildings and structures). More recently it has been applied in an adapted form to the procurement of design services (see 'Fee bidding' p. 20).

The selective search

The traditional procedure for selecting an architect involves the client in some form of search. Various methods are used but in general a shortlist is drawn up based on advice and recommendation and the client's own knowledge and experience. The shortlisting can be followed by visits – to the architects' offices and to their completed buildings – and by interviews. Architects are sometimes asked to outline how they would approach the particular project but, until recently, few clients required designs to be drawn up because this cost them money (fees were payable in accordance with the published RIBA scales).

The architectural competition

The architectural competition system enables the promoter to consider a number of designs.

The key elements of the architectural competition are that the winner be selected on the basis of design quality alone and that all competitors work to the same instructions and criteria. The submitted material is assessed by a jury. The fee arrangement is established at the outset. Procedures are drawn up to ensure that these objectives were met. (A detailed description of the architectural competition process is given on page 43.)

Each of these methods is designed to serve a particular end. The tender process provides the client with a price for the job, established on a competitive basis. The selective search provides the client with an architect, with the expertise to develop the design and the experience to see the project through to completion. The architectural competition provides the client with a design, worked out to a given brief and examined by experts.

Taken together, these three systems can be seen as providing ways of securing the 'best' price, the 'best' architect and the 'best' design. If they could all be rolled into one in some way, the client would then, perhaps, have the perfect procurement system. The weakening of the professional institutes' controls and influence, the abolition of the fee scales and the impact of the recession on the workload, left the market open for some of these 'all-in-one' procurement ideas to be tried out.

Current competitive formats

A whole range of 'hybrid' competition procedures is now being used. They take elements from two or, sometimes, all three of the traditional formats, the procedures of one system being interwoven with those of another. This more flexible approach has introduced some interesting and productive ideas into the selection process. But problems occur when the pick and mix approach involves taking different parts of an integrated system without considering the original role or intent or assessing the effects of the change.

Fee bidding

This is a system where the selection of the architect and/or design team is made solely on the basis of how much they would charge to do the work. The competitive element is one of price. The term 'tendering' is increasingly used in this context as the process derives from the application of the traditional tender system to the commissioning of design services.

The client sets out the stated requirements and invites competitive fee bids for design services. The architect or team putting in the lowest price for the required design service is appointed to carry out the work. In most cases some checks are made as to qualifications, experience and financial viability before bids are examined.

Fee bidding can only work effectively when it is made in a response to a full and detailed specification. Those bidding for the job can then make an assessment of the amount and complexity of the work required and clients can compare like with like. Experienced clients control the process carefully. They ask for a detailed specification of the service offered including the number of hours to be worked and the names of the design team members on each part of the job. Regular audits are carried out to ensure that the work is undertaken in accordance with the agreed specification.

Commissioning through the fee bid is not a method which encourages designers to spend time questioning the brief or exploring alternative solutions. It lends itself to projects where there is a standard design solution and where significant elements of repetitive work are acceptable.

There are problems related to this approach and various groups within the construction industry are looking at methods of regulating current practice, both in respect of tendering for design services and for works. The main concern is that the system does not necessarily secure 'value for money' in the longer term. Those who oppose its use argue that fees buy design time and that the time invested in the initial stages of a development is crucial to the long-term success of the project. They also claim that the nature of the design process is such that any cuts which are made in the time spent overall, tend to be concentrated on the initial design stages.

Clients are worried that the tender process may not even guarantee the lowest price in the short term. The downward pressure it places on prices, fees and potential profits leads to suppliers finding methods of disguising some of the costs until the contract or commission has been secured.

Although presented as an option for the procurement of services in the EC directives, several countries in the European Union do not regard it as applicable to the commissioning of architectural services. Opponents of the system in this country cite practice in the United States of America where the Brooks Bill forbids public works to be allocated on the fee bid system. The bill was introduced in 1972 to further the interests of public accountability and to guard against incompetence and corruption.

Procuring architectural services on a fee bid basis is one of the few competitive procedures which can readily be identified as lying outside the orbit of the architectural competition on the basis that no design work is required in the bidding process.

Compulsory competitive tendering (CCT)

The system seeks to regulate the processes by which local government authorities allocate work to in-house providers. Legislation has been introduced to cover a range of provision including architectural and other design services. A proportion of all such work is required to go out to some form of competitive tender.

This is a form of 'fee bidding' and as such introduces the concerns and considerations set out above as well as problems relating to an incompatibility between price and quality based assessments. The RIBA has expressed 'serious doubt whether quality in creative design services can be specified in a way suitable for price competition'. The government is exploring a number of procedures designed to safeguard quality standards. These include the concept of a 'quality threshold' and the introduction of a 'dual envelope' system (one envelope containing a bid on quality, the other a bid on price).

CCT is not a form of architectural competition. Its application relates to the cost of the design services not the quality of the design.

Design and build

Here the competition is between developers or building contractors rather than architects. It is a growing area with an increasing variety of procedures. In essence, the client (the person seeking a building) invites proposals in response to an outline brief. The developers, working with their own in-house or consultant design teams, prepare a bid which includes both a design and a price for the completed job. The system has its roots in commercial developments but is now used for a whole range of building projects. (The term 'package deal' is sometimes used.)

In some situations, the client establishes the financial base at the outset and then seeks developments which work within the given parameters. An alternative approach is for the client to set out the requirements (e.g. office accommodation or a leisure facility) and look for the best solution in terms of quality of design, lowest cost or some form of value for money amalgam.

Views are mixed about the effectiveness of many of the methods used. Like many other forms of procurement, the design and build system has met with problems over recent years. The University of Reading's Centre for Strategic Studies in Construction is currently (1995) studying 250 design and build projects, in order to work towards guidelines for better practice. The study is partially funded by a client consortium (including Tesco, Marks and Spencer and the National Westminster Bank), and aims to draw on the experience of architects, engineers, building material suppliers, lawyers and management consultants.

Whether or not this system falls into the category of an 'architectural competition' is debatable. Attempts have been made to draw up formats to regulate its use and it remains an option in the current RIBA system though one which is very rarely used. (RIBA competition documents refer to the process as 'Design and bid: developer/architect competititions'.)

The case study on page 144 looks at a design and build competition (for a housing development for the London Borough of Brent).

Design and fee bid

This system operates on the basis of a simultaneous assessment being made both of the design and of the cost of the design fees (not the project cost). It relates to the concept of assessing 'value for money'. The process is also referred to as 'tendering'.

The system merges elements of the 'tender' process with that of the architectural competition. A briefing document is issued and architects and design teams are invited to respond with designs and associated fee bids. In some cases an initial invitation is published and responses are invited from any qualified person or team. In others, the brief is sent to a pre-selected group of perhaps four or six practices. The aim is to identify the designers who can both provide the best solution to the brief and work to the lowest cost. Where this does not prove to be an option, the promoter can follow one of several courses. One way is to select the best design solution (setting it aside if the fee is out of line with all the others). Another possibility is to go for the lowest fee bid (rejecting it if the design is unacceptable.) Obviously there is a temptation to try to get the best of both worlds, i.e. to select the most interesting design solution and to beat the fees down to those of the lowest bidder or to pick the cheapest designer and ask him/her to incorporate aspects of the preferred option.

The use of the system is widespread. Some clients claim that it works well but it is resented by many architects who regard it at best as a lottery and at worst as a form of exploitation. When they are in a position to choose which competitions they enter, architects try to avoid the fee bid situation. Much of the current criticism of competitions stems from these design and fee bid contests.

The following problems are inherent in the process:

- Competitors do not know on what basis they are being judged, as neither the quality of the design nor the cost of the fees is set as the main criteria. Those who enter have to make a judgement of the promoter's real intent. If they get it wrong, the work they have done is wasted.
- Architects are often expected to prepare the designs without any payment through the (false) analogy with both the tender system (which is designed to put a cost on a clearly defined set of requirements) and the architectural competition system (which is designed to explore quality design solutions in accordance with an agreed set of procedures).
- 'No fee' design work tends to be rushed and undertaken only to secure the commission. The danger is that the next stage of the design work has to be put in hand quickly and undertaken on a low-cost basis, allowing no time for problems to be thought through and sorted out.
- The widespread use of the 'design and fee bid' system has led to a vast increase in abortive design work. If architectural practices are to operate on a financially viable basis, the cost of this design work has to be recouped in some way. There are two ways in which this can be done: one is to load the fees charged on work which does go ahead and the other is to cut back on the overall service provided. Neither of these can be regarded as in the long-term interests of the clients.

Procedures based on the 'design and fee bid' system are not generally considered appropriate to a system of architectural competitions where the objective is to secure design quality.

Design and negotiated fees

A system which many architects and clients find more acceptable is one in which design selection is followed by fee negotiation. By separating the design assessment from the cost considerations, the problems inherent in the simultaneous assessment of quality and price are avoided. The separation of these two elements is regarded as crucial in any form of architectural competition.

One way of operating is as follows: when designs are submitted a statement setting out the fees required to develop and implement the design is placed in a separate envelope and detached from the main submission. The proposals are assessed either on the basis of the work submitted or in direct discussion with the architects. The envelope containing the fees for the winning design is not opened until after the final selection has been made. Fees are negotiated and the winning scheme is only set aside if no agreement can be reached. There is some discussion as to whether or not the promoter should be permitted to open all the envelopes. Some people think that this leads back to the fee bid situation. Others consider that the formal separation of the two elements provides sufficient safeguards.

Where fees are to be the subject of negotiation the sealed bid system can work to both the promoter's and winning architect's advantage. As there is no fee bidding element in the selection procedure itself, competitors can be expected to put in fees which relate directly to their design proposals. Variations in fees should reflect the complexity of the design work involved and the levels of service offered.

This procedure can be used in conjunction with an architectural competition provided that the basis on which the architect is to be appointed (i.e. the fee negotiation) is stated in the competition conditions.

The University of Durham competition, described in the case study on page 168 incorporated a negotiated fee procedure.

Design/designer selection methods

The traditional selective search involved shortlisting on the basis of experience and expertise followed by visits and interviews. The design/ designer selection methods follow this procedure closely but instead of relying on looking at previous work in order to assess the architects' design skills and potential compatibility of approach, clients now ask for designs or design approaches to be produced.

Once design work is introduced into the selective search it takes on many elements of the architectural competition. For design work to have any relevance, it has to be produced in response to some form of brief and assessed against that brief. The competition system has been developed over the years to provide an equitable and effective format for selecting a design on this basis. It is not surprising, therefore, that the design selection procedures which are regarded as 'best practice' incorporate many of the principles of the architectural competition.

These selection procedures may be directed towards securing either the design or the designer. Where the competition format is followed, this distinction seems to be more a question of emphasis than of objectives or procedures. In explaining the 'designer selection method', its proponents claim that it enables the promoter to make a design assessment without by-passing the 'dialogue' stage of the design process. In theory, the appointed architect is free to amend or completely change the approach once the appointment has been made. The design work is only required to 'test' design skills with the real work of developing the brief beginning once the selected architect has been appointed. In practice, design work requires a brief and the winning architect or team is selected on its design response to that brief. Most clients would expect the appointed architects to follow the approach which led to their selection. The distinction between a competition to select a designer and one to select a design may be more readily understood if it is seen as relating to the stage to which the design is developed and the amount of detail required rather than to a different basis of selection. (The RIAS follows this approach.) Seen in this way, it enables a line to be drawn between design-based competitions and selective search methods which introduce an element of design work into the process of choosing the 'architect for the job'.

In practice, the objectives of securing the right architect and of identifying the best design approach can become intertwined. The selection methods in current use bring in interviews, presentations and discussions at a number of key points. Interviews are used to select, shortlist or check on capabilities and attitudes. Presentations are used to aid design assessment. Meetings and discussions are used for briefing purposes. Some design selection methods follow the selective search procedures with all the decisions remaining with the client. Others take the form of an architectural competition and involve a jury.

Those who support the use of these procedures as part of the competition system, claim that they are the best way to secure design quality. They argue that the ultimate quality of a design is inseparable from the ability of the designer to develop and implement it and that both sets of skills need to be tested at an early stage. They do not believe that these skills can be adequately assessed on the basis of drawings and reports considered in isolation. For this reason the procedure includes briefing, interview and presentation sessions.

The format can work well. One of its strengths is that it adapts to suit the individual promoter's requirements. Where these are to secure a design of the highest quality, the design selection method allows the promoter to introduce a range of selection procedures directed towards this end. Where the promoter has other aims, the system is equally adaptable. Used insensitively or inappropriately, it leads to many of the problems listed under 'Design and fee bid'. The promoter needs to have technical expertise and a good understanding of the design process to use these methods effectively. First time clients would be well advised to appoint an architectural advisor or use the competition system.

In adapting the traditional architectural competition to respond to changing requirements, interviews and presentations were also introduced into this system. Some RIBA competitions, and to a lesser extent those promoted by the RIAS, are now virtually indistinguishable in format from the competition-based design selection method.

The procedures used in the design/designer selection method are not, however, universally accepted as being appropriate for architectural competitions. The international systems do not allow any contacts between promoters/assessors and competitors. The EC rules for 'design contests' also preclude interviews, presentations and briefing seminars during the competition process (see Chapter 9).

The South Bank Centre case study outlines the selection method used to appoint a designer – the 'master planner' (see page 176). The case study for the National Trust's Langdon Cliffs competition demonstrates how the selection method can be used to find a design (see page 153).

Ideas competitions

One of the traditional distinctions which is continued in the current systems is that between project competitions, where there is both the intention and the commitment to build, and ideas competitions, which are promoted as exercises in design. Ideas competitions are hardly mentioned in this book. This is intentional. Though they share a common name and many procedures, the basis on which they operate is quite distinct from that of the project competition. Ideas competitions are designed to stimulate discussion. They require an open brief which encourages exploration and innovation. The aim is not one of identifying practicable and realisable solutions for an intended project.

An ideas competition is a design exercise. It is often used to look at different ways of using a building material, to focus attention on the potential of a site or to explore approaches to a particular building form. In this country they often have a promotional intent (e.g. the Architectural Student Award promoted annually by British Steel).

Occasionally, the ideas competition format is used (or possibly misused) to select a design for an actual building project. In such cases, no commitment is made, because the promoter has no funds with which to proceed. The competition is promoted as a fund-raising exercise. One of the most publicised competitions run in this way was that for the Dulwich

Picture Gallery extension (1990). It attracted 921 enquiries and 377 submissions. To date, no progress has been made with implementing the winning design.

The issue is an important one in relation to the distribution of lottery funding. In many cases, the promoter will only be able to build if his or her lottery bid is a successful one. This does not, however, preclude a commitment being made to appoint the winning architect (and pay the design fees incurred in preparing the competition winning design). Recent lottery competitions have tended to follow the project competition format but with the 'commitment to appoint' clause adapted to take account of the lottery element.

The competitive interview

In reviewing its competition system, the RIBA Competitions Committee started to explore the concept of a 'competitive interview' in which selected architects are given an outline brief and, after a period of study, return to be interviewed and present their (illustrated) approach to the problem set. The stated intent is to help inexperienced clients with the process of selecting an architect (not of securing a design). It seeks to regulate existing practice and to limit competitive work. It can also be seen as an attempt to find a competitive procedure, acceptable to the lottery funding bodies, which does not require architects to develop outline designs in order to secure a commission.

The 'competitive interview' could prove an effective method of selecting an architect (the current equivalent of the selective search), but it is questionable whether it has a place within the architectural competition system. It would certainly not fulfil many of the other objectives of those pressing for increased use of architectural competitions.

The competition dilemma

Most of these formats depend on the architectural profession carrying out design work for which there is no (or at the best a very much reduced) payment. The traditional architectural competition system confined this within a carefully controlled and regulated system, used on an occasional basis for a specific set of purposes.

Competitive work has now become part of the normal process of securing a design commission. The design work required can take a scheme to a stage which, if the architect were appointed, would attract a fee in the region of 15% of the total design costs. When this amount of work has to be put in to say ten schemes in order to get one commission, the problems are obvious.

This is the dilemma which faces the architectural profession in considering what to do about competitions. There is a measure of agreement about the main objectives. Fee bidding is not regarded as in any way compatible with design quality and pressure will continue to exclude those procedures from the procurement system. Clients will also be encouraged to use procedures which are both equitable and professional, whether they follow the traditional architectural format or use the more flexible design selection method, and to provide adequate safeguards for those who take part. But even if these objectives could be achieved and all competitions proved to be well-run and assessed on quality alone, there would still be a problem.

The architectural profession, taken as a whole, does not consider that it can carry the cost of extensive competitive work and wants clients to consider other ways of securing design quality. Many architects would like to see a system based on the 'selective search' with clients being prepared to commission on the strength of experience and previous work. Architectural competitions should not, it is argued, be used every time a client wants to choose between one architect and another.

At the same time, it is evident from the continuing debate on the subject, that the competition system has some very influential supporters. They maintain that there is a crucial role for the architectural competition. What this is and how it can be developed is explored in Chapter 4.

4 Competitions – who needs them?

With so many different competitive processes being used, the unique qualities of the traditional architectural competition and its current equivalents are becoming blurred. In its 1986 guidelines, the DoE describes competitions as 'a challenge to those who promote them, widening choice, forcing thought to be given to the objectives being sought, yielding better designs through the help of experienced judges'. The catalogue for a recent exhibition on competitions held at the RIBA Architecture Centre (October 1994) included the following statement:

> Taken individually, RIBA competitions encourage new design thought about a particular building type, encourage fresh architectural talents to emerge, and offer promoters a variety of concepts to consider. Taken together, competitions offer a critical comment upon the architectural thought and expression of a period.

The RIAS competition brochure describes architectural competitions as 'vehicles for the release of creativity, vitality, new talent and new ideas'. Documents produced by the Finnish Association of Architects describe the competition system as creating 'opportunities for renewal and change in the built environment. Competitions open the way to the art of architecture and creative freedom, though within set rules and programmes, and through disciplined and expert procedures.'

A different style of commissioning

What is so special about an architectural competition? It is evident that when the term is used in the statements quoted above it refers to something other than the process by which two or more architects compete for a job. When pressing for a wider use of the system, its supporters are certainly not asking for more clients to invite more practices to prepare even more detailed design work before they consider offering a commission. What they want is to introduce a different style of commissioning into the procurement process.

The difference lies as much in objectives and intent as in procedures. The aim of the architectural competition system is not just to offer clients a wider choice nor to distribute work more evenly throughout the profession (though it can do both these things). It relates to the development of the art and science of architecture. The objective is to open up the commissioning process and introduce a whole interplay of different interests and in so doing encourage debate, discussion and exploration. 'It is the peculiar, special and temporary relationships of the promoter, the architect, the jury and the public which constitute the essence of the architectural competition' (RIAS exhibition catalogue, *Winners and Losers* 1991).

While drawn together during the process of a competition, each of these participants has its own particular set of interests. Some of these are complementary, others are conflicting. Architectural competitions depend on concepts of reciprocity being established and accepted. Each of the participants has to make some concessions in return for balancing safeguards. If all the safeguards are on one side and all the concessions on the other, the system cannot function effectively. While no system can ensure that everybody is satisfied all the time, procedures need to take account of the multiplicity of interests and endeavour to achieve a constructive balance. Co-operation and goodwill are essential elements.

Defining the interests

The client

The competition system offers the client choice and the opportunity to extend the boundaries in which that choice is exercised. The introduction to the RIAS exhibition catalogue outlines the context:

> The promoter may have a variety of reasons for contemplating an architectural competition, not all connected with architectural quality or even architecture. The shotgun effect of multiple-entry competition may produce the one hit that solves the problem of a difficult site or an impossible brief (they do exist!), acts as a catalyst to raise funds or awareness, reassures public or established opinion, confers prestige on a pedestrian enterprise or, indeed, achieves great architecture.

In gathering evidence for this book, questionnaires were circulated to competition promoters. The target group was limited to RIBA and RIAS competitions (where the rules have to adhere to the principles of the competition system) and covered the decade 1985–94 (these are listed in the Appendix). One of the questions asked was: 'Why did you decide to hold a competition?' Responses were varied. Some promoters regarded themselves as patrons, others as discerning clients. Some used the competition system to meet their own criteria, some to satisfy those of other people.

A city authority promoted a competition 'to maximise public involvement in the choice of design and to broaden the scope of design ideas'.

The head of an independent school replied, 'To let us see a range of innovative and different designs.'

A local authority technical officer wrote, 'The problem was converting an existing poor building to accommodate a range of activities which required specialist work.'

An arts organisation wrote, 'We decided to hold a competition to obtain the best quality design possible within our available budget. As promoters of good practice we believed that Architectural Competitions are the fairest way of identifying appropriate practitioners to design buildings.'

A local authority replied, 'The Council-owned land lay on the edge of a Conservation Area with unusual topography and the site had been reclaimed from industrial use. The intention was to inject a higher standard of quality and design than the market would otherwise have achieved in this location.'

A developer responded, 'the site is of national importance ... it was necessary to appeal to the Secretary of State. At appeal, consent was given to demolishing the existing building on the basis that we held an open international architectural competition for its replacement. When the site is very sensitive or the local authority is unable to come to a decision, it can be of assistance to the promoter to take a step back and let the best ideas come to the surface. Unfortunately there are time and cost penalties. It is not an appropriate method for selecting regular, run of the mill buildings.'

These clients have all identified the system as being appropriate to a particular set of circumstances. Similarly the case studies in the second half of this book demonstrate that when clients take the trouble to run a well-organised and carefully briefed competition, they use the system discriminately. It is recognised that it is not a way of getting designs 'on the cheap'.

Promoters who follow good practice guidelines – their own or those drawn up by the professional institutes – resent suggestions made by some architects that they are getting 'something for nothing'. The managing agent for one such competition (praised by those who took part) writes:

The criticism levelled at architectural competitions (*Building Design* Editorial) is that generally architects do a lot of work for little return whilst clients secure a lot of work at little cost. It is probably clear from the schedule of documentation that our client committed a good deal of time and effort to this competition. Our costs (i.e. management, prizes, consultants' fees, etc.) represented a small part of the real cost incurred by the client in terms of in-house time and resources. It is my opinion that we offered architects adequate and appropriate information at the preliminary proposal stage to allow them to decide if they wished to take part. Architects are professional people who should be capable of weighing the pros and cons of a competition.

Competitions open the doors to new ideas and new people. In one sense this is not a 'safe' process, which is why a system of guidelines and supporting structures is required. For the client, a building involves a long-term commitment. Firstly, they want a building which fulfils their requirements and, secondly, they want a project which is completed on time and within budget. When selecting the designer through competition, they need a system which they can trust. Not all clients want to be involved at every stage (some recognise that there can be advantages to 'stepping back' from the selection process) but they do need to be assured that when they delegate decisions, their interests are served. Most clients are spending other people's money – public funds, shareholders' investments, trust funds – and feel they have a duty to be cautious. Lord Crickhowell, chairman of the Cardiff Bay Opera House Trust explained the gap between the announcement of the result and the acceptance of the competition winner as follows: 'Over the last few weeks, the trustees have been seeking to make sure that we had all the facts to make sensible decisions and to avoid the disasters that have befallen so many construction projects in the past.' The Cardiff Bay competition had been very carefully run and assiduously assessed. Lord Crickhowell got the assurances he was seeking.

Many clients find the process of promoting an architectural competition to be a rewarding one. Opening up briefing procedures to a wider range of interests (board members, staff and users), tends to draw people together and make them more willing to contribute towards a common objective. The interchanges within the client organisation and between the client team and the professional advisers (in both the briefing and assessment stages) can lead to a better all-round understanding of the issues involved and a more constructive approach to the whole project. One such 'user' (a staff member invited to join the assessment team) expressed enthusiasm about the whole approach: 'It felt like a luxury with people listening to what we wanted – not like all the argy bargy we had in the past where you had to spend so much time to get even the smallest thing changed.'

The architect

Architects share a common objective in wanting to limit unregulated competitive work and ensure that competitions are properly run. But when it comes to making suggestions as to how the architectural competition system should be organised, their different interests become apparent. The profession is divided on the issue.

Architects work increasingly in a commercially-based market (private and public sector alike). To operate profitably they need to attract fee income for the design work they do. In this context, direct commissions can be seen as serving architects' interests best. Any system specifically designed to identify new talent (i.e. potential competition for future commissions) cannot be regarded as a commercially attractive proposition.

Some established practices want all appointments to be made on the basis of an architect's record of work. Architect Ian Salisbury, for instance, is quoted in an article which appeared in the *RIBA Journal* (August 1994): 'The best way to procure a building is to choose an architect on experience and reputation and negotiate a brief and design for the purpose required.' Where competitions are held, these architects want invited competitions with a limited number of participants (figures as low as four are quoted as being desirable).

There are other, equally well-established practices, who want to see architectural competitions form an integral part of the procurement system. Their preference is for two-stage open competitions and limited competitions, provided the limited competitions offer some opportunities for new talent to break through. Practices which have made their names through success in architectural design competitions are often strong advocates of the system when it is used to offer opportunities to younger and less well-known practices. Many of the competition advisers and assessors are previous competition winners. They do not, however, support a system in which they are required to compete with one another for any and every major commission. There is evidence that these architects are now declining some invitations and it is rumoured that a process of 'sharing' (you go for this one, and we will try for the next) is being introduced as the workload increases. They feel that their practices' skills and approach are sufficiently known for many selections to be made without recourse to design work.

Younger architects and less established practices still hope for more open competitions to be promoted, preferably organised in two stages to limit the amount of work required from unsuccessful competitors. (At present, only one or two competitions a year offer genuine opportunities to this group.) These architects think limited competitions are only acceptable, on a general basis, if some way can be found of enabling younger or newly-established practices to compete. They cite the system which operates in Germany, France and Holland where winners of open competitions are invited to take part in subsequent limited competitions and would like to see similar opportunities offered in this country. Their voice is heard less frequently than that of their older and more established colleagues for the obvious reason that they are not on councils and committees and tend not to be consulted very often. They have to rely for the most part on their more influential colleagues 'remembering what it was like' and speaking on their behalf. One young competition-winning practice describes its situation as follows:

> We set up about five years ago. The practice has been funded by other work – consultancy for other architects, teaching, etc. We managed to get onto one invited competition through the publicity given to the first win. The biggest problem is the lack of competitions – those which are held are so over-subscribed.

Architects practising outside the London area are wary of competitions which take away design opportunities in what they regard as 'their patch' especially when they go to a selected and predominately metropolitan group of architects. They prefer smaller projects to remain within the area, either through an invited competition or one limited to the architects in the region. This is not as narrow minded an approach as it may appear. European experience has shown that regional competitions can help to strengthen a region's design base, enabling younger architects to stay put and build up practices based on design quality.

Although winning the commission is the primary objective, architects have a secondary agenda. They see competitions as providing welcome opportunities to explore new themes and extend their areas of expertise, make bids for new types of work, demonstrate their design skills, and attract public attention. One competitor, asked why he entered competitions, summed it up as 'Good fun, good experience, it got us out of a rut for a while'.

Public aspirations

The competition debate has tended to focus on the roles of the architect and the client. This is changing. There are other groups waiting in the wings eager for something more than a walk-on part. John Gummer, Secretary of State for the Environment, set the scene in his opening speech at the 'Quality in Town and Country' conference (January 1995): 'Architecture is the most public of arts. Each time a builder builds he is performing a civic action . . . he is not just building for his customer.'

Katherine Shonfield, writing in *Building Design* (20 January 1995) about the veils of delusion which hang over the competition debate, sets out the following proposition. 'Delusion 6: A competition is a fair and democratic way to give the public what they want. A competition is simply . . . a puffed up glorification of the private relationship between architect and client. Where are the elected representatives of public interest?' There is evidence in many areas that the public is beginning to claim its interest in what is built – for its use, in its name or with its money (British taxpayers spend £4 billion a year on buildings). This interest is frequently expressed as opposition but where organisations take the trouble to explain and consult, the interest can be turned to something more constructive.

When the subject of procurement is being discussed, the client tends to be represented as an autonomous individual who makes a personal decision as to what best suits his or her needs. This does not adequately reflect the facts of the situation. The client for a building for public use is more likely to be an appointed Board of Trustees (who may change with the government) or a group of managerial staff (who may not be there when it opens). It could be argued that these people hold the building in trust and work on others' behalf and that, as custodians rather than owner occupiers, they have a duty to consult the wider constituency of interest.

Despite Katherine Shonfield's 'Delusions', the competition system is about the only procurement method which can be organised to provide opportunities for public consultation and participation – not to 'give the public what it wants' but to give people an opportunity to contribute towards the decisions which shape their environment and to learn about the processes involved. Richard Rogers and Mark Girouard write:

> A contest catches the imagination . . . the public can look, learn, comment, write and agitate if it feels like it, make its input as the project moves from winning entry to final design and help create a climate of opinion which will affect future competitions.

The competition criteria, the shortlisting procedures, the composition of the jury, and the development of the selected schemes are all legitimate areas for public interest. A number of promoters who have moved in this direction on their own inititative have met with some success, but on the whole the opportunities are neglected. The procedures by which such involvement can be encouraged and turned from a potentially damaging process to a creative and constructive one need to be identified and developed.

Accountability

The sleaze debate which rumbled on throughout 1994, focussed attention on the potential for corruption in public life and led to more consideration being given to how decisions are taken and money distributed. One of the aspects of the current procurement system which people find worrying is that it provides very few safeguards against vested interest, it allows the operation of cabals and exploitation (on all sides) and offers even fewer incentives to provide quality in design and building.

The official competition system and those competitions which follow its principles and procedures, provides an open and regulated format for selecting a design. This could be a determining factor in favour of using the system when public funds are being distributed or where controversial or potentially valuable planning permission is being sought.

Access to opportunities

There is a strong current of opinion developing which maintains that where public money is being spent, contracts should be distributed on an equitable basis. It is argued that public commissions should be spread amongst suppliers rather than being concentrated in one particular area or on a single individual or company. This is one of the objectives which the EC service directives are designed to secure.

All architects are qualified to design buildings. If the principle of equal access to available opportunities is to be followed, systems are needed which select either on a random basis (ticking suppliers on the list of those qualified as they receive commissions) or on the basis of stated criteria. The competition system is one method of distributing work fairly and equitably on the criteria of 'design quality'. It can be demonstrated to work effectively, provided that its principles and procedures are followed.

The quality of architecture

Architecture is a creative process which needs opportunites for ideas to be explored, for standard approaches to be tested, for discussion to take place, and for expertise to be shared. One of the ways this can be achieved is through an architectural competition.

There are parallels to be drawn with other art forms. Systems exist to encourage theatres to provide opportunities for new writing and for orchestras to include new works in their repertoire. The Arts Council's funding of competitions, through its lottery money, could provide similar opportunities for architects.

This role of the architectural competition can perhaps be best seen in an historical perspective. Architectural writer and historian, Peter Blundell Jones writes:

> For the critic or historian, competitions have quite a different value as a barometer of the current state of the art, providing opportunities to compare different ideas and approaches on the same ground. The various approaches are all buildings that might have been and show us different worlds. In comparing them we see all the great coercive power of architecture which is normally hidden in the false inevitability that a building takes on once it is realised.
>
> (*Architects' Journal*, June 1976)

What sort of projects?

There is no evidence to suggest that any building type is inherently unsuitable for a competition. When architects talk about projects being 'inappropriate' for a competition, they are often referring to circumstances (e.g. lack of funding, existing conflicts about what is required, reluctant client, etc.) which make entering it a risky enterprise. But what one group considers to be 'inappropriate' could be the motivation for another.

The case studies show that the system can be made to work for a wide range of projects in terms of scale, usage and ownership. Those who recommend its wider use identify the following situations:

- where projects are funded (either in their entirety or in significant proportion) by public funds;
- buildings, regardless of sources of funding, which are for public use or which impinge on the public domain;
- major projects, including large schemes which affect the structure of towns and cities or which make a significant impact on the environment;
- high profile schemes in key sites or areas of special interest or significance;
- individual buildings which are representative of a type in order for different approaches to be explored and new ideas to be tested.

This list, if applied across the board, could cover a large proportion of all new building work. Given the concern which the architectural profession has about 'an excessive extension of competitive work' and the additional costs which a competition places on the client, the list probably needs to be seen as referring to situations where some form of architectural competition should be considered rather than required.

Where a project is a significant 'one-off', when the site is of particular interest either regionally or locally, where the project is the result of a co-operative effort or has to meet the requirements of disparate groups, where some special expertise is required – all these are situations where a competition could provide the best solution. There is also a strong case to be made for competitions to be promoted on an occasional basis to bring new ideas into standard building forms.

The need for a co-ordinated system

Several attempts have been made in the past to establish the promotion of architectural competitions more firmly within the commissioning process in this country. Although the UK was one of the first countries to draw up competition regulations, its system has not met with the success of those run, for instance, in Scandinavia or Germany or, more recently, in France.

The relative success achieved in these countries owes much to their internal structures – the relationship between central and local government, the importance of the regions, the autonomy of different levels of government, the role of the city authorities – and to the aspirations and attitudes of the particular cultures. It also relates to the way the design professions are structured and design work organised. These relationships, attitudes and structures cannot be picked up and transported wholesale into another country merely to encourage the more extensive use of competitions. It is possible, however, to identify some common features which make the difference between a competition system which is integral to the process of obtaining new buildings and one which is peripheral.

A successful system involves a certain number of architectural competitions being promoted on a regular basis. By holding competitions, organisations learn to run them more effectively. By becoming involved in the design process the public learns how to use it to its advantage. By competing for commissions on the basis of design quality, architects sharpen their design skills and their skills of presentation (both to the client and the public).

The process is a cummulative one. Once a pool of competition expertise has been developed, promoters find it easier to identify which schemes are appropriate for competition and what procedures are most likely to work well. Competitors can be more selective, identifying the projects which are most suited to their experience and approach.

It is not even necessary to promote a competition to appoint a competition-winning architect provided that there are sufficient opportunities for these designers to become recognised. Exhibitions help competition winners to become known; publications showing winning designs enable promoters to select architects with the appropriate design skills.

This is what is meant by a competition culture. When competitions are seen as 'one-offs', a series of isolated events, as they are in the UK, much of their potential value is ignored. Considered as an integral part of the procurement process, the system can be used to serve a range of objectives. It can share out work on the basis of talent, identify gifted young designers and help get them established, support and develop existing practices, and retain and strengthen the design base of a region or area. In terms of the practice of architecture, competitions can be used to develop skills, concentrate attention on difficult problems, explore design ideas or direct attention to alternative processes. The system has a role in stimulating and educating public interest. To achieve these objectives, it needs to be co-ordinated in some way. It requires the expertise to be shared and the experience gained in each competition to be passed on.

Recent experience shows that having more competitions does not of itself secure a thriving competition system. As demonstrated in Chapter 3, there are hundreds of competitions (i.e. several architects preparing designs for a single project) being held every year in this country. In most cases, very few people even know they are being held. User and public participation is limited or non-existent; there is no exhibition so no comparisons can be made and the criteria on which the selection is made are known only to those directly involved. The years 1994 and 1995 have also seen a marked increase in the number of large scale architectural competitions. In the main, these competitions have been for an invited group (whether or not an initially open invitation was made). Nearly all of them have been restricted to already known and established practices while some have been used to select only from amongst 'famous names'.

If architectural competitions are to serve the objectives set out above, a system needs to be developed which encourages a range of competitions to be promoted: open, limited and invited; large, medium and small; international, European, national, regional and town or city based. There is a case to be made for having a few competitions to select from amongst the established stars and for having rather more to identify the stars of the future. The thrust of any co-ordinated competition system, however, needs to be directed towards providing initial and continuing opportunities for the talented and competent. Architectural competitions need to extend a client's accepted commissioning base. Techniques which rely on exclusion – either of ideas or people – at an early stage, work against the very principles the competition system is designed to serve.

The competition challenge

In the past, the professional institutes took responsibility for administering the architectural competition system, offering regulated sets of procedures to those who chose to use them. It is evident from the small number of architectural competitions they have run in the UK (rarely more than ten in any one year from the RIBA and RIAS combined) that this has not proved to be an effective way of developing the desired 'competition culture'. One reason used to be that clients felt that the system was designed to protect the architects' interests and that its use was imposed on them. With the institutes' control of competitions gone, architects are now complaining about the problems they face when the clients pick up the competition procedures and adapt them to suit their purposes. Neither architect- nor client-led competitions would appear to provide a sound base on which to build an effective competition system. Where several different groups have an interest in a process, there is a strong case for each of them to be involved in its development and regulation.

There are examples of this happening in other countries. In Holland, the competitions co-ordinating committee includes representatives from eight different arts and design organisations. In Finland, the competition regulations are endorsed by both architect and client bodies. In France, the whole process by which architects are commissioned for public works is regulated (mainly through a system of architectural competitions) by an interministerial government organisation. In this country, an analogy could be drawn with the Joint Contracts Tribunal and National Joint Consultative Committeee which regulate practice within the building industry. The difference is that the public also needs a voice in how the architectural competition system is organised.

The challenge facing those who want to see an effective system operating in this country is to find a way of moving from the current situation – one of unregulated competitive work and unco-ordinated competitions – to that of the 'competition culture'.

One of the problems facing those who try to encourage more open competitions is that initially these competitions will attract a very large response. This puts people off using the system. Not only are these 'over-subscribed' competitions difficult to handle and wasteful of time and resources, but they also tend to distort the design process by putting pressure on competitors to produce attention-claiming designs in an attempt to both attract the interest of the assessors and 'justify' the competition to the promoter.

Once there are a sufficient number of open competitions, the situation will begin to regulate itself. But until the open architectural competition becomes more established within the procurement process, some more controlled form could prove the better option. There are two main ways of controlling entry – one is to select and the other is to limit eligibility (see Table 4.1). Competitions which select six or so entrants can work very well in terms of matching the design to the project, but they tend to exclude the architects

Table 4.1: *Preferred criteria for participation in limited competitions*

Architects were asked to indicate preferences for eligibility:

Previous experience	██████████████████
Geographical	████████
Practice size	███
Age (e.g. under 35)	none
Competition/award winners	██████
Next in line (from a registered list)	████

which the competition system is designed to support. If invited and limited competitions are to work within a more integrated system, ways need to be found of widening the selection base. The case studies on pages 153 and 160 demonstrate how two different client organisations approached this issue.

The most obvious way of limiting eligibility is on a geographical basis (provided the projects do not fall within the jurisdiction of EC regulations or remain below its threshold limit). There are many arguments to support a regionally based competition system for small scale projects. They strengthen the regional design base, encourage solutions which respond to the locality in which the scheme is to be built and develop a greater public awareness of design issues by focussing attention on known and local projects, as well as ensuring that the architect is 'on hand' throughout the design and building stages.

Once the expertise has been established at this level, it provides a base on which a more wide ranging use of the system can be built. Architects who have proved their skills (both in design and implementation) stand a better chance of being selected for larger projects. Clients who are familiar with the regional system feel more confident in using an architectural competition for a major scheme. The RIBA Competitions Office began to develop a regional competition system at the end of the 1970s. It met with some success but fell into disuse in England when the central support weakened and the regional network was allowed to disintegrate. The idea at that time was for RIBA regions and branches to administer a very simple format which could be used for smaller projects. The system could be adapted to suit current requirements, though more widely-based regional co-ordinating groups might be considered appropriate to the 1990s.

At the end of his series of Reith lectures (BBC radio, 1995), Sir Richard Rogers calls for a government-led initiative 'to involve citizens in the problems of their environment':

> The Victorians built public libraries, we should build architecture centres. The architecture centre is where the planning committee would meet in public. It would become the focus for public debate on strategic plans, planning applications and competitions. It would also hold lectures, exhibitions, courses and debates.

Some form of government initiative could well prove to be the most practical way forward. It is unlikely to take the form of prescriptive legislation – merely mentioning the possibility is enough to launch an attack on the whole concept of architectural competitions. But the government might consider it to be in its interests to fund the crucial first steps, documenting and publicising how the architectural competition system operates and working with other interest groups to establish enabling structures. The Architecture Centres movement could provide the base on which to build.

Competition agencies

The Royal Institute of British Architects
66 Portland Place, London W1N 4AD. Tel: 0171 580 5533.

The RIBA has a detailed and fully documented competition system, the basis of which is shown in the chart on page 44. The RIBA offers advice and consultancy as well as a full management service. It organises competitions on a regional, national or international basis. Initial information is available through the RIBA Clients Advisory Service.

The Royal Incorporation of Architects in Scotland
15 Rutland Square, Edinburgh EH1 2BE. Tel: 0131 229 7545.

The RIAS has considerable experience of running competitions and providing advice to promoters. It organises competitions on a regional, Scottish, UK wide or international basis. Information is available from the RIAS Competitions Unit.

The Society of Architects in Wales, 75a Llandennis Road, Rhydpennau, Cardiff CF2 6EE (Tel: 01222 762215 and **The Royal Society of Ulster Architects**, 2 Mount Charles, Belfast (Tel: 01232 323760) may be approached for initial information.

The International Union of Architects
51 rue Raynouard 75016, Paris. Tel: 010 331 45 24 02 78.

The IUA provides a system for organising international competitions which is fully documented in several languages (including English). It provides a co-ordinating service and will nominate competition managers and assessors.

The Architecture Foundation
30 Bury Street, London SW1Y 6AU. Tel: 0171 839 9389.

The Architecture Foundation offers an advisory service on competitions. The Foundation is a charitable trust dedicated to the development and understanding of architecture. It has no documented competition system but has been involved in a number of major competition projects including those for the South Bank Centre and the Tate Gallery (both in London). Its competitions tend to follow the designer selection method.

5 Principles and procedures

The Department of the Environment guidelines for competition promoters (published in 1986 but now out of print), opened with a definition of what distinguishes a competition from other forms of commissioning.

Four criteria are listed:

- there are several entrants;
- there is an identical problem set for all entrants;
- rules and procedures are prescribed and followed;
- systematic and independent assessment by a panel of assessors is used to select a winner.

There are two principles which can be regarded as providing the foundation for the whole system of architectural competitions:

- the panel assesses the quality of the design against criteria established in the brief;
- the whole process is conducted in a fair and equitable manner.

The 'rules and procedures' which are used in the various competition systems organised throughout the world all aim to define structures which incorporate these two principles. In the past, they did so through standardised formats and sets of model competition conditions. Increasingly, these are being replaced by guidelines setting out good practice procedures.

Architectural competitions follow a basic pattern. A brief is drawn up which sets out the promoter's requirements. Competitors are invited to respond to the brief in accordance with a set of intructions specifying the type, scale, size and number of drawings and accompanying material to be submitted. An independent panel of assessors is appointed. A proportion of its members are architects and/or other suitably qualified members of the design professions. The panel works on the principle that the entries are judged on the basis of the material submitted and are assessed against the criteria established in the brief. The technical requirements may be checked by specialist consultants. The panel makes its decision and reports to the promoter who proceeds to commission the architects responsible for the winning design on the terms set out in the competition conditions. Prizes are awarded and payments made in accordance with the published rules. A public exhibition is held of competition entries.

Architectural competitions can be open, limited or invited. They can be run in one or two stages. They can look for a design approach or a more fully worked proposal. All architectural competitions, whatever their country of origin, share these common attributes. The choice of competition types and procedures offered by the RIBA is summarised in Figure 5.1.

The current UK systems provide opportunities for the final selection to be made by the promoter and for interviews and discussion meetings to be held at certain stages in the selection process.

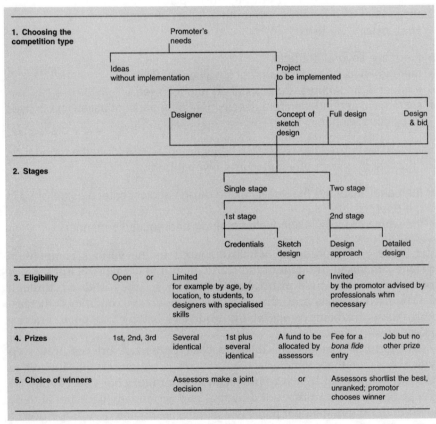

Figure 5.1 *Choice of competition type and procedure. Reproduced by permission of the copyright holders. Copyright RIBA Publications 1986*

The information given in this chapter draws on accepted practice, published guidelines and current experience. It does not seek to define any particular competition system.

The competition team

In some forms of procurement the client, as an individual or managing group, appoints the design team and works with them to determine requirements, develop the brief, explore solutions, test possible proposals and work out the agreed design approach. In a competition roles are divided and a group of people are drawn together to carry out a number of distinct and specific tasks.

The competition manager

All competition guidelines recommend that a competitions manager is appointed well before any detailed preparation is put in hand. Even where the promoter has experience in commissioning and has a strong internal technical team, a competition manager will be needed to co-ordinate the competition process.

The manager is responsible for the whole organisation of the competition. The job includes establishing the framework and drafting the rules; appointing and servicing the assessors and technical advisers; organising the brief (either writing it or commissioning an experienced team to do so); preparing and distributing the documentation; ensuring the required level of entry; providing a point of contact for competitors; arranging any meetings, seminars, discussion or visits which are required; co-ordinating the assessment procedures; stimulating and responding to public interest; dealing with the press and media; mounting the exhibition and handling the announcement of the result.

The manager could be an individual or an organisation. Both the RIBA and the RIAS offer a full management service. Most organisations which provide project management would also be prepared to advise on and manage a competition. (Not all of them have the necessary expertise or experience so checks may need to be made.)

The costs of competition management relate to the size and complexity of the project, the scope of the competition and the range of services required.

The panel of assessors

The competition system is based on a concept of assessment by an independent jury. This is one of the principles of reciprocity which underlie the system – architects work on a design problem so that a range of solutions can be explored. They do so on the understanding that the selection will be made on the basis of the quality of the design solutions submitted and that the assessment will be undertaken by people who have the experience and expertise to recognise that design quality.

In the traditional architectural competition this need for independent and professional assessment was interpreted as requiring an architect-only jury, nominated by the appropriate professional institute. This proved unacceptable to most promoters. The system gradually accommodated greater promoter involvement in the assessment process, sometimes with parity and sometimes with majority representation on the jury. The present RIBA requirement is for two architects on a jury of four (the 'preferred' – not mandatory – jury number) while the RIAS looks for 'adequacy of peer assessment'. Many European countries and the international system require the professional assessors to be in the majority. The EU directives ask for one-third of the jury members to hold the equivalent (as a minimum) of whatever design qualification is demanded of competitors.

While flexibility is now the keynote of the UK systems, the principle of professional and independent assessment still underlies discussions regarding jury composition. Establishing the right balance between architects and non-architect assessors is also regarded as important to the judging process. Once again it relates to the concept of developing a design through 'dialogue'. The architect assessors work with those of other disciplines and backgrounds to test out the ideas against the promoter's requirements.

Jury numbers vary considerably. International competitions can have as many as twelve assessors with others sitting in on the process in case one of the appointees collapses half way through (or is forced to withdraw for other reasons). The UK systems favour a smaller jury. The RIBA-recommended jury of four aims to achieve the desired balance while enabling the assessment to take place on an informal, almost conversational level. Small juries are considered to make each assessor feel more responsible for his or her decision. In large juries, it is argued, the assessors are more likely to follow a strong lead and then feel less committed to the result. This argument appears to be based on anecdotal evidence, sufficiently endorsed by individual experience for it to be passed on. One disadvantage of a panel of four is that it could involve the chair in a casting vote. (With the 'promoter choice' option, the RIBA requires the chair to be one of the architects. In all other RIBA competitions formats he or she is one of the assessor's representatives.) Other systems avoid anybody having a casting vote by specifying that juries comprise an odd number of people. The chair tends to go to the most senior representative of the promoting body.

The selection of assessors is one of the key decisions to be made when a competition is being organised. Traditionally, the promoter delegated the decision to the jury. Although the promoter is now more closely involved in the selection process, and may well make the final decision, the assessors are still responsible for judging the merits of each entry against the brief and advising the promoter accordingly. Picking designs at the stage where concept and potential are all important is a difficult task requiring experience as well as expertise. For this reason, the professional institutes seek to match an assessor, selected for a particular knowledge of the design type, local area, etc., with an experienced competitions assessor.

Sherban Cantacuzino, then Secretary of the Royal Fine Art Commission, is quoted in an article by Paul Barker (*Perspectives*, January 1995):

> The crucial decision is to appoint the jury. If you want a Classical building, set up a jury that is likely to award it to a Classisist, and those people will apply. Of course, the opposite is much easier, because most architects are modernists.

Promoters need to be aware that their choice of assessors can send messages to the competitors. The main message, however, relates to the seriousness of the promoter's intent and the status of the competition. Where a particular architectural style is required, it is both fairer and more effective to state the preference in the brief.

Both the RIBA system and the EC directives for design contests require the jury to be independent. This could be defined in one of two ways. Either the majority of the jury should be unassociated with the promoter or the jury, whatever its composition, should be free to reach its own decisions.

Questionnaires were sent to architects asking them to rate the factors which they considered important when looking at the composition of a competition jury. Recognised expertise was generally regarded as more important than either an independent majority or an architect/designer majority. The key factor seemed to be the quality of the decision making – judged retrospectively. If the competitors perceive bias in the selection of the winning architect or team, they will then criticise the composition of the jury for not following the independent design majority formula. The operative word here is 'perceive'.

Promoters are recommended to appoint assessors early in the competition process, as they have a contribution to make to the way the competition is organised. In the RIBA system, one of its nominees is appointed as the senior architect assessor. This person will have competition expertise and will be able to advise the promoter. The senior architect assessor would expect to be consulted on the competition documents and could be commissioned to write the brief.

The professional institutes have a set scale of fees for the assessors which they nominate. In all other cases, the fees are a matter of negotiation between the promoter and the assessors and would normally be calculated on the basis of the day rate payable for the commensurate level of consultancy.

Some promoters do not bother with a jury of assessors – they shortlist, interview and select. Whether this is a 'rogue' competition or just some other form of selection (on the grounds that, by definition, a competition involves independent assessment by a jury) is a matter of opinion. Competitions run in this way may not attract the best level of entry. For example one competition-winning architect said he was 'very wary' about all-client juries: 'I am not touching that one – I just don't trust it.'

The financial adviser

Where a competition is intended to lead on to a building project, it is essential that properly worked out cost limits are set in the brief and that the winning design meets these cost requirements.

The financial adviser, normally a quantity surveyor, needs to be appointed before detailed work on the brief begins. The promoter has to ensure that the cost limit is a realistic one, both in terms of the amount of money available for the project and in terms of that figure being adequate to cover the requirements set out in the brief. Competitions have gone wrong in the past because the cost target was set at an unrealistically low level for the space, facilities and quality required in the brief.

The financial adviser joins the technical team during the selection process. In most competitions, competitors take independent advice from the quantity surveyor of their choice, who would normally be seen as part of the design team. The winning architect would expect the team which worked on the competition design to be appointed as consultants for the project (see page 58). Occasionally, the promoter specifies that his or her financial adviser will become a member of the design team. In this situation, there is a case for making the services of this adviser available to competitors during the competition process.

The technical team

Technical consultants are brought to advise on the brief and to check submissions.

Most building projects require the advice of a structural engineer. A number of other consultants can be brought in to make up the team of technical advisers. Who they are depends on the project. They could include planning and landscape specialists, design consultants, people with commercial or industrial expertise or those with specialist knowledge relevant to the competition.

Technical advisers should be appointed at the outset of the competition so that they can contribute to the brief. They may also be involved in question and answer procedures and briefing and selection interviews. During the actual assessment process they normally work as a team checking specific aspects of the submitted designs and reporting their findings to the assessors. How they operate depends to a certain extent on the wishes and requirements of the panel of assessors. They may check all the entries before the jury meets, work alongside the assessors to advise on specific points as they arise or be called in to look through an intitial longlist (i.e. a selection of 15–20 schemes). The technical team is asked to comment but is not expected to exclude, shortlist or place the schemes in any order of merit.

They are normally paid on the basis of the amount of time they spend on the work.

User and interest groups

There is a growing interest in using the competition system to widen the basis on which the selection is made and to draw more people into the process. Some promoters extend the panel of assessors to bring in staff members, user representatives, local amenity groups, artists and writers. Others keep the panel small but bring together an advisory group which works in the same way as the team of technical advisers (i.e. checking their particular area of concern or expertise and reporting to the panel of assessors).

In most situations, the second method is likely to prove the better option. It allows wider interests to be considered while concentrating the assessment on the overall 'quality of design' criterion.

There is considerable scope for consulting user and interest groups and the general public when the project is first being considered and when the competition brief is being prepared. There are no standard procedures recommended, though various methods have been used successfully in the past. The case studies outline some of the methods followed.

Basic competition procedures

There are a number of procedures which are integral to the architectural competition. They are there to serve a given set of objectives.

The question of anonymity

Decisions about anonymity are not an 'add-on' once everything else has been decided. They determine which type of procedure is followed and how the selection is carried out. The traditional architectural competition system required complete anonymity to be observed throughout the whole of the competition. This is retained by the international and multi-national competition systems and is a requirement of the EC directives covering 'design contests' (in order to ensure that considerations of nationality are kept out of the assessment process).

Complete anonymity throughout the competition process is intended to ensure that decisions are made on the basis of the quality of the design alone. To preserve anonymity, the assessment and the management have to be quite separate processes. Some competition procedures require that even the contact between the competition manager and the competitors is conducted through a third party nominated by the competitor (i.e. if the competitor wants to know that his entry has been received they must include a stamped enveloped addressed to a friend, relative or colleague). If any form of pre-selection is made, all those designated to take part in the judging have to be excluded from this initial selection process to ensure that the names of competitors are not known to the assessors. All entries are submitted 'without name, motto or identifying mark' and accompanied by an 'official competition envelope' in which the completed entry form is sealed. In RIBA competitions, the manager puts a number on each of the drawings and related material and on the outside of the competition envelope of each entry. In international (IVA) competitions, competitors are asked to make up their own six figure number (as the lottery demonstrates, there are not many duplicates). The assessors identify the submissions by their numbers both during the judging process and in their report. The envelopes are only opened once a final decision has been made and recorded. The Durham University competition was organised on this basis (see Case study 8, page 168).

The advantage of this system is that it is transparent and can be seen to be scrupulously fair. It minimises the potential for accusations of bias or manipulation to be made. It ensures that all architects are given equal opportunities to demonstrate their design skills, analysing the problems set in the brief and presenting design solutions. Some would argue that 'anonymous' competitions offer the best opportunities for younger architects.

When observed to the letter, the anonymous system precludes any form of contact between the assessors and the competitors. This could be seen as a disadvantage on two counts. Firstly, it does not allow for any discussion of the brief or any exchange of information outside of the written documentation. Some people find that direct discussion leads to a better level of mutual understanding – of the promoter's requirements and of the competitors' proposals. Secondly, it is perceived as providing few safeguards for the promoter who fears an inexperienced or 'difficult' winner.

Most competitions held in the UK introduce some interview, discussion and presentation procedures into the briefing and assessment processes. In some cases, anonymity is still observed throughout the design assessment part the process. This is achieved by using the pre-selection and/or promoter choice options. Pre-selection of competitors allows the promoter to exclude those who cannot demonstrate that they have the experience to carry the project through to completion. This could prove a useful option for some projects but, if too restrictive in its approach, the pre-selection could exclude those most likely to bring new ideas and approaches to the design problem. An alternative is to use the 'promoter choice' option where the panel of assessors shortlists two or three winning schemes. The competition is regarded as having been completed at this stage and it is then open for the promoter to select whichever architect or scheme is preferred. This enables anonymity to be preserved throughout the whole of the competition process while providing a safeguard and choice for the promoter. The RIBA Competitions Office considers that this system fulfils the EC requirements for a design contest.

Some people question whether true anonymity can be maintained. They argue that design is not a bland concept particularly where quality is concerned. If one architect's approach was really indistinguishable from another's there would be little point in holding a competition. Just as literary critics can make a fair guess at the author of a piece of text, the sort of architects normally chosen as assessors have sufficient knowledge of their field to distinguish between the design approaches of different colleagues and to make a fair guess at indigenous and foreign work. By the second stage of a competition (or throughout an invited one), the architectural grapevine usually ensures that the names of many of the shortlisted competitors are known. Guessing which entry goes with which architect provides a bit of competition for the assessors.

This is only a real concern where there is a known or all-star cast. This is rare in competitions which start with an open invitation and proceed to shortlist on design criteria alone. The 'all star' or 'all-known' situation usually results from initial shortlisting on this basis. It is part of the design/ designer selection method (which does not seek to follow anonymity requirements) rather than the traditional architectural competition.

Competition advertisement

The invitation to take part in an open competition usually takes the form of an advertisement. A major project could be advertised in one or more of the daily newspapers. Most promoters rely on the technical press. Where the RIBA and RIAS manage a competition, they handle the advertising for the promoter. The RIBA has recently introduced a competitions newsletter circulated on a subscription basis. Some larger commissions now have to be advertised in the *EC Journal* (see Chapter 9).

The purpose of the advertisement is to attract the right level of interest for the competition. It needs to give enough detail for architects to assess whether or not the project is a suitable one for them. Where the invitation is to be followed by some form of pre-selection, the criteria on which this selection is to be based should be set out in the advertisement (e.g. 'experienced design team', 'with specialist knowledge of ...'). Where a project is subject to EC directives, these criteria have to be stated – otherwise the client is bound to shortlist on a random basis or appoint on lowest price. In other cases, it is in the promoter's interest to limit the response (and the work in handling it) to those who stand a chance of being selected.

Entry requirements – eligibility

Entry can be open or limited. Open competitions usually extend the invitation to all qualified architects, with other design professionals and students free to enter provided they do so in association with a qualified architect. While UK law does not require buildings to be designed by architects, it does define the term 'architect'. (The Architects' Registration Council, ARCUK, regulates this.) Reciprocal recognition of qualifications has been negotiated and the term 'architect' is now defined throughout the European Union.

There are various ways in which entry can be limited. Restrictions can be set in terms of area (architects living or practising in a particular country, region or town); age (e.g. architects under 40); or status (newly-established practices, or multi-disciplinary teams). Limiting entry by experience or expertise normally involves the promoter in some form of checks and pre-selection as these terms are open to interpretation.

Registration

It is normal practice to require competitors to register for a competition. The procedure is that they pay a fee which entitles them to receive the competition documents and be placed on the official list of competitors.

Originally promoters asked for a deposit, returned to those who submitted a 'bona fide' entry. This system was found to be both costly and difficult to administer and so was replaced by one involving a small but non-returnable fee. The size of the fee required has grown as it has come to be seen as a source of income sufficient to cover the cost of producing the documents. Intending competitors can now be asked to pay up to £100 to find out whether they are interested in entering a competition or, in some cases, to register to be considered for inclusion (e.g. when first-stage competitors are selected from an initial trawl).

There is a case to be made for reviewing this practice, especially when registration does not automatically entitle the architect to enter the design stage of the competition. A simply produced document setting out the terms and conditions, would enable architects to make a decision without having to send for the full sets of conditions. The South Bank Centre, for example, relied on its advertising, circulating additional information only to the selected competitors (see page 176).

Competition stages

Traditionally competitions were either 'single-stage' or 'two-stage' depending on the complexity and scale of the project or on the amount of detailed design work sought.

In open architectural competitions, the two-stage is now the norm. A single-stage format tends to be used only for invited competitions or those where some form of pre-selection is made. At the same time, all competition procedures are becoming more flexible. Some of the design/designer selection methods appear to go through a gradual and continuing process until no further options remain. Even a standard RIBA two-stage competition can begin to look like a four-stage process when pre-selection is included and 'promoter choice' follows the assessors' decision.

One of the 'good practice' principles in the competition system is that promoters ask for the minimum amount of design work required to make an informed decision. The purpose of staging is to limit the amount of design work required from competitors until the odds are shortened and the schemes showing the most potential have been identified.

The staging system also aids the judging process. It can be difficult to assess (and even to handle) a large number of entries where they are all taken to a detailed design stage. When a competition is organised in two stages, the first stage can be used to identify key points. The second stage tests and develops the initial approach. The system also gives the assessors a chance to comment on the first stage designs and give additional briefing to the competitors. The first stage could, for instance, show that certain routes are just not worth pursuing or that several promising designs need to tighten-up on particular aspects.

The only disadvantage to staging which promoters identify is that two-stage competitions take longer. Where a quick result is crucial some form of pre-selection would normally be regarded as preferable to a single design stage requiring extensive design input.

Selection procedures

In recent years a variety of different selection procedures has been introduced to complement the process of assessing design submissions. In the systems which follow the traditional architectural competition, these tend to be kept separate from the design assessment. In the design/designer selection method they are integral to it.

Pre-selection, long- and short-listing

Promotors are increasingly looking for ways of limiting the entry, either by some form of pre-selection or by placing restrictions on who can enter (preclusion). In some cases, promoters first preclude and then select. Whether or not all the methods used are acceptable within the terms of the EC procurement directives is open to interpretation (see Chapter 9).

Pre-selection is normally made on the basis of relevant experience. Architects and designers are invited to submit information about their qualifications and expertise and about the work they have already carried out. They can be shortlisted on the basis of this information alone. In some cases, promoters draw up a longlist and reduce it following visits and interviews (the case study on page 153 outlines this approach). There is a case to be made for promoters taking a more eclectic approach at this stage in the competition. The competition system is designed to provide choice and to do so within a structure which safeguards the client's interests. It offers opportunities for standard solutions to be tested and new approaches to be developed but these opportunities are limited if the promoter selects on the basis of 'only those who have already designed two or three of the same thing'. (The case study on page 160 demonstrates an alternative approach.)

Where 'expressions of interest' are invited good practice requires that:

- some initial information is provided (preferably free of charge);
- the pre-selection criteria are clearly stated;
- the information which competitors are required to submit is strictly limited and excludes design work.

Some competitions ask everybody who is interested to register, to study a detailed brief and to submit a report outlining their approach. If the subsequent shortlist demonstrates a strong preference for a particular type of practice or is limited to well known and established practices, other would-be competitors resent the time and money they have been required to spend.

First- and second-stage selection

The selection procedures vary according to the competition approach. In the traditional architectural competition the decision is reached solely through consideration of the material submitted. The assessors judge the entries against the published brief. The winning design is expected to be the one which, in the opinion of the assessors, best fulfils the promoter's requirements as set out in the brief. The following procedure is used.

The numbered entries are set out on screens or tables. With a large entry it may not be possible to display all the drawings together – a system of display and replace has to be used with entries going into a provisional reject or reconsider pile as appropriate. Assessors find it advisable to go through the reject pile again before the final shortlisting takes place. Sometimes the merit of a particular approach only becomes apparent after a number of schemes have been studied. At some stage in the proceedings, the technical team studies all the entries (or a longlist selected by the assessors) and prepares a report (see page 48).

The assessors meet as a jury. They may work individually and then confer or they may maintain the team approach throughout the whole process. Most juries follow a system of comparison and exclusion rather than attempting to pick the winners. They go through the entire entry, taking out schemes and backchecking from time to time, until they are left with a list of possibles. This process continues until a few more than the required number remain. The assessors then debate the merits of the remaining schemes, voting, if necessary, to establish the final shortlist. In the first-stage selection, entries which take an interesting approach or show potential for further development may be included. By the second stage assessors have to be convinced that the winning scheme is technically sound in all major respects and is capable of being built within the established cost limit.

Sometimes the choice of winner will be an obvious one but on other occasions a number of schemes could be seen as having equal merit (and possibly balancing shortcomings). Individual assessors may champion different schemes. The system requires, however, that the jury reaches a decision which, if not unanimous, is accepted by all its members.

Many of the competitions now being promoted introduce interviews into the selection process. Those who follow the traditional format most closely separate the interviews from the assessment of submissions. The first-stage assessment is carried out as described above but the assessors are asked to produce a slightly longer list of competitors than is required for the second stage. The competitors are then interviewed (by the assessors, the promoter or some representative group) and the second-stage competitors are selected on this basis.

The design/designer selection procedure style of competition integrates interviews and presentations into the selection process. The procedure outlined in the conditions for the Tate Gallery Bankside competition (1994) demonstrates one way of operating:

> Up to fifteen practices will be selected to participate in Stage 1. They will be invited to join a tour of the site in order to supplement the information contained in this document (the brief). The tour will be followed by an opportunity to meet the staff at the Tate Gallery at Millbank. [The submission requirements are then listed]. . . A principal from each practice will be asked to present their ideas to the assessors during a presentation and interview session. Forty-five minutes will be allowed for each competitor, with the presentation taking no more than 20 minutes.

Various types of meeting, including interviews, are also used for briefing purposes. In principle, selection and briefing are distinct processes. In practice, some mingling of objectives is probably inevitable.

Final selection

Traditionally, responsibility for the whole selection process lay with the panel of assessors who were required to select an outright winner. Increasingly, assessors are asked to shortlist two or three potential winners and prepare a report setting out the reason for their choices. The promoter (as an individual, board, council or committee) invites each of the competitors on the final shortlist to attend a meeting to present their schemes and answer questions. The assessors and technical advisers are usually present to advise the promoter.

This 'promoter choice' option was introduced into the system to counter accusations that a winner could be foisted on an unwilling promoter. Whether or not this system is used depends on the initial objectives of the competition. There are situations when the aim of the competition is to delegate the selection process. The promoter choice option obviously introduces an element of subjectivity into the selection of architect. The 'best' design will not necessarily be chosen as the outright winner. Received opinion is that where one architect is far more well known and established than the others, he or she will be awarded the commission. It has also been claimed that it is possible to manoeuvre a competitor through to this stage on the grounds that most juries would concede one favorite scheme to a determined group of the promoter's assessors.

But the system has the advantage that it encourages the promoter to identify with the choice of winner. Having made the final selection, the promoting body (board, council, etc.) is far more likely to support the winning scheme. In practice, the system appears to work effectively. Where there is an obvious winner (i.e. one which demonstrably fulfils all the criteria of the brief far better than any of the others), the promoter is unlikely to cast it aside. Where there are several equally good schemes or where all the selected schemes have some minor problems, it could be considered appropriate that it is the promoter who makes the final decision.

Rewards, commitments and incentives

The competition system works on the basis that the interests of each participating group are respected. The promoter is presented with a range of design approaches. In return for the time given by the architects, certain obligations are placed on the promoter (see Table 5.1).

Appointment of winning or selected architect

The purpose of a competition (other than an ideas competition) is to identify an architect or design team to carry out a particular commission. The main

Table 5.1 *Relative importance of different factors in the competition system*

Competition criteria: analysis of architect's responses

- no importance
- minimal importance
- quite important
- very important

Assessors How important is it that the jury . . . ?

- is identified at the onset
- has an independent majority
- has an architect majority
- has recognised expertise

Other factors How important do you consider the following to be?

- amount of prize money
- guarantee to appoint winner
- firm intent to build
- copyright safeguards
- anonymity throughout
- anonymity in first stage
- exhibition of all entries
- publication of results

reason people enter competitions is that they want to secure the job on offer.

The official systems all require the competition to close with the appointment of the winning architect. The relevant RIBA model clause reads as follows:

> The author of the design placed first by the assessors (or selected by the promoter from the assessors' shortlist, in the case of the promoter choice competition option) will be appointed as the architect for the work. If the promoter does not wish to go ahead with the scheme, the winning architect is paid the design fees due (the first prize rarely reimburses the architect for the amount of design work undertaken in the course of the competition) and the process is at an end.

Some promoters seek to avoid making this commitment. Whereas they would recognise their obligation to pay an architect they had commissioned to carry out design work, they do not consider they have the same obligation to pay for the work if it has been 'commissioned' through the competition process. If you call it a competition, the argument goes, you do not have to pay anyone. This misrepresents the competition system. Within the established competition system, the conditions always required that the winning architect be paid for the work done – the first prize being regarded as an advance of fees due on appointment.

The competition procedure does not officially end at the point where the winning design is selected. It continues until the architect is appointed. It is this commission which brings the competition to completion and the promoters' commitment to a close.

Appointment of design team

In larger competitions many promoters now specify that they are looking for the design team rather than the architect alone. In cases where a team entry is specified, the commitment to appoint the authors of the winning design would be interpreted as referring to both the architects and the consultants.

Virtually all project competitions require other consultants to be brought in, especially in the second stage. It is common practice for these consultants to work with the architect on the basis that they will be appointed should their scheme win. If a promoter is not prepared to consider the design team recommended by the winning architect, this should be made clear in the competition conditions.

Prizes and other forms of payment

Winning prize money is not the main incentive for those entering competitions (even ideas competitions) but it does play an important role in validating the process. It is part of the balancing of interests – an investment on the part of the promoter which serves to demonstrate good intent.

The allocation of prize money depends on the format of the competition. In a single-stage competition it is usual to allocate money for three prizes – either first, second and third or three equal amounts. In invited competitions and in the second stage of a two-stage competition good practice requires that each competitor receives an 'honorarium' – a payment slightly less than the third prize. This compensates competitors in part for the detailed work carried out. It should be a large enough sum to both cover the expenses involved in preparing the submission and make a contribution towards the cost of the design time put in. This 'good practice' procedure can be seen as working in the interest of both architect and client. One promoter, responsible for commissioning architects on a regular basis, confirmed that all the entrants in a recent invited competition for which he had been responsible, had received a payment. He took the view that it had served to reinforce the architects' commitment to the project: 'I wanted their quality time – their bright-eyed Monday morning time – not the clapped out time they might manage to squeeze in over the weekend.'

The amount of the prize fund and the way it is to be distributed should be set out in the conditions. (There may be a sub-clause which allows some of the money to be redistributed at the discretion of the assessors.) In some invited competitions, the prize fund is distributed equally amongst all the competitors except for the winner whose 'prize' is the commission. In others a 'pool' is made available for the assessors to distribute at their discretion.

The prize money offered needs to relate to the size of the project, the amount of detailed work required and the impact the promoter wishes to make. Prizes in international competitions tend to be higher than those in the UK, so promoters need to raise the stakes if they want to attract a significant international entry. The case studies give details of the prizes offered in each competition.

Copyright

In the UK system copyright remains with the authors. In some countries there is a system by which ideas can be 'purchased' through special competition awards. This is not the situation in this country and neither the promoter nor his or her consultants have any legal right to use the ideas from the competition submissions – other than those of the winning design once the architect has been appointed.

The right to publish and display the drawings is normally established in the competition conditions.

Announcement and exhibition

The competition system has a number of objectives other than that of securing a high quality design. It demonstrates a range of different design approaches, enables comparisons to be made between one proposal and another, focusses attention on architectural problems and opportunities and identifies new design talent. Whether or not these objectives are achieved depends very much on the attitudes of the individual promoters. If the promoter merely takes the winning design and ignores the fact it was achieved through a competition, much of the interest of the process is lost.

All the established competition systems require that a public exhibition is held. While they recognise that not all promoters are prepared to show every entry, they do ask that all the second-stage submissions or all the submissions in a limited or pre-selected competition are displayed. The Cardiff Bay Opera House Trust showed drawings and models of the second-stage entries, and made a 'wall' (a display case) of all the smaller scale first-stage models with the other material in boxes (as in shops selling prints) so that it could be studied by those interested in getting an overall view of the entry. The 'wall' is shown in the Frontispiece.

Making an event of the announcement or exhibition opening attracts attention to the results of the competition and provides publicity for the prize-winning and shortlisted schemes. Having a public exhibition demonstrates the open nature of the selection process and the effort made to secure the best solution.

Documentation and briefing procedures

The DoE description of a competition gives one of its criteria as 'there is an identical problem set for all entrants'. The problem – the issues which the promoter requires competitors to address – is detailed in the competition brief. The procedures through which solutions are to be offered are set out in the competition conditions.

Competition documents

The competition documents comprise the conditions (the rules by which the competition is to be conducted); the brief (detailing the promoter's requirements); supporting information (e.g. location and site plans, consultants' reports, site surveys, planning context, etc.) and procedural items (e.g. entry form, official envelope, cost pro-forma). These are sent to all registered competitors and form the basis on which the whole competition operates.

Competition documents can be expensive to design and print. This is not a mandatory cost. There is a marked difference in quality (in terms of typesetting, paper weight and the amount of colour printing) between the documentation produced by the RIBA for the competitions it manages and those produced by some of the more high profile independent promoters. Whether the more expensive form of presentation contributes to the overall success of the competition is debatable though these promoters may well consider that the additional expense is justified in terms of both clarity of presentation and of the competition image.

Drawing up the competition brief

The development of the brief is a continuing process. The work starts well before the competition is launched and continues after the winning architect is appointed. (The processes involved in drawing up the brief are outlined in Chapter 6.)

A competition requires that the brief is defined at some point in this process and presented to the competitors in a way which enables them to explore a variety of possible routes forward. The point at which the competition brief is fixed depends on the nature of the problem and the amount of detail being sought. The South Bank Board, for instance, was looking for a development plan for the Centre and its surroundings. The brief concentrated on problems and expectations (Case study 9, page 176). The Trustees of The Richard Attenborough Centre for Disability and the Arts were interested in design details as well as the overall approach. The brief they issued specified the spaces and facilities required (Case study 4, page 137).

The purpose of a competition is to extend choice and open opportunities. A competition brief has to make the promoter's requirement clear by providing the information the competitors need without closing off potentially productive routes of exploration. Competitors are given a range of information on which to base their designs. The brief needs to make the status of this information clear: whether it is provided as background or whether it specifies the established approach; if it is mandatory (i.e. any competitor who does not fulfil the requirement will be disqualified) or discretionary (desirable but left to the competitors to make their own decisions); whether it is a priority or low down on the list. Problems occur when promoters make requirements which they subsequently decide are unimportant or add a supporting document which then turns out to be a key study.

In two-stage competitions it is usual practice to issue the full brief at the beginning of the first stage. In most cases, however, the assessors will initially be looking for a few key factors which determine the approach. The brief should state these main criteria clearly.

Additional briefing documents can be circulated at the beginning of the second stage of the competition. These should not change the established requirements (as this could invalidate some of the competitors' work). Assessors often use this second briefing opportunity to draw attention to important aspects of the brief or to add information.

The brief is crucial to the whole success of the competition. It spells out the promoter's requirements. If it is inadequate or flawed in any way, this will be reflected in the quality of the submissions. One of the key principles of the competition system is that the submissions are judged against the brief. This means that any scheme which does not meet the criteria set out in the brief has to be disqualified. If the promoter has got the brief wrong, there is no opportunity for competitors to make suggestions to put it right. They have to respond to what is there, not what they think should be there.

Written questions and answers

Where anonymity is being observed, competitors are invited to send any questions they may have to the competition manager (this procedure is occasionally omitted because of pressure of time or where the promoter wants to leave options open). The competitors are normally allowed about one month to study the conditions and begin to work out outline approaches before the 'last date for questions' deadline is met. This procedure may be used in both stages of a two-stage competition.

The manager lists all the questions and, in consultation with the promoter, assessors and technical advisers, circulates either a set of answers or a report covering the main issues raised. All competitors receive the same information, that is questions are answered collectively not individually.

Additional briefing procedures

Increasingly, promoters are introducing procedures which allow more direct briefing to be given. The written question and answer system is often supplemented by a discussion meeting (variously called a symposium or colloquium) to which all competitors are invited to send one or two representatives. The assessors and technical advisers (and possibly consultants and specialist staff) are usually present. A tour of the site or existing buildings (in the case of a conversion) may be included. Obviously, this system is not appropriate in the initial stages of a large open competition.

The colloquium system is sometimes used to brief the second-stage competitors in a two-stage competition. In some cases, promoters have introduced one-to-one meetings at the beginning of the second stage at which the individual approaches are discussed. Some people find this procedure unacceptable in that it goes against the principle that all competitors are given exactly the same information. Others consider that it can help in directing a scheme away from a potential blind alley and concentrate the competitors' work on the aspects which demonstrate most potential. One competitor comments, 'the opportunity to visit the existing facilities and meet the client to discuss the first-stage submission was invaluable. These meetings enabled the client to understand the design approach and the design team to respond to client's comments and requirements.'

Where this system is used, promoters have to take care that any information which could be regarded as additional briefing material is given to all competitors.

The assessors' report

Once the panel has reached a decision, it reports back to the promoter setting out the terms of its award (i.e. first, second and third prizes or best three, etc.). The assessors are usually expected to prepare a written report setting out the reasons for their decision. Most official competition systems require that this report is published. It is part of the transparency of the selection process. The report provides a critique of the competition and entries. Its publication is part of the sharing of experience and mutual learning process which many consider to be one of the key points of a competition system.

Submission requirements

In describing how competitions should be run, the term 'level playing field' is often used. This refers both to briefing procedures and submission requirements. To ensure that all submissions are judged on an equal basis, the competition conditions set out exactly what material each competitor is required or permitted to submit. The conditions state what drawings are required (e.g. plans of all principal floor levels and sufficient sections and elevations to explain the design) and to what scale each of them is to be drawn. It is normal procedure to specify both the number and size of sheets on which the drawings are to be submitted. (It is advisable to check that there is a correlation between the number and scale of the drawings, and the size of sheet specified.) Some form of report is often included. Where this is required, it is usually defined in terms of both the page size and number of sheets.

Good practice (and the practicalities of assessment) require that the design work is kept to the minimum amount and detail needed for an informed assessment to be made. In some cases an illustrated report might be regarded as sufficient in the first stage of a two-stage competition or for a selection based on a design approach. Examples of submission requirements are given in the case studies.

Most competitions state specifically that 'no models are to be submitted' but many permit photographs of models to be included in the report. Where models are required it is normal practice to limit them to small scale, simple block models to show the massing of the building and/or the position on the site. The Cardiff Bay Opera House Trust Competition, for example, included a template card in its conditions with the requirement 'a block model in white at 1:1000 scale should be provided on the site template issued with these conditions'. The template fitted into the promoter's model of the site and surrounding area which helped the judges assess the scale of the proposed buildings and how they related to their neighbours. The same system was used by the Museum of Scotland (see Case study 3).

Where submission material is not specified in this way, judging can be extremely difficult as like is not being compared with like. Competitors could feel pressured into working to excessive detail. This not only places uneccessary burdens on entrants, it also means assessors have to plough through long reports and sheets of drawings in order to work out exactly what is proposed and how well it meets the requirements of the brief.

The need for ease of comparison should be borne in mind when specifying submission requirements. Competitors are often issued with site plans and cost and accommodation pro-forma to ensure that they are all working to the same basis.

Promoters also have to be aware of the potential problems in handling and storing large numbers of competition entries. Competition submission requirements normally spell out such details as whether or not the drawings are to be mounted, how this is to be done, whether landscape or portrait formats are to be used, etc.

Where presentations are part of the selection process, most promoters specify the time allowed and the display techniques to be used. Where well-established practices are in competition with smaller organisations, it is important that the level of presentation is specified and kept within reasonable cost limits, if only to prevent accusations being made (should the large practice be selected) that the assessors/promoter were unduly influenced by an expensive presentation.

6 Failures and fiascos: can they be avoided?

Working out requirements and getting a project designed and built is a time consuming and complicated process. There are a whole range of things which can go wrong along the way – some of which could result in the project being abandoned. In some cases things go wrong because of poor planning or management, in others because of changed circumstances. Competitions are not immune from these problems nor do they necessarily contribute towards them. Architects looking down the 'outcome' column in the list of RIBA competitions held between 1985 and 1994 (see page 183) will recognise a familiar pattern of events. An analysis of any set of projects over this period wil probably identify a similar range of 'completed', 'pending' and 'abandoned' schemes. The explanations given in this list for projects not proceeding to completion may include the odd polite cover story glossing over a major bust up but on the whole they give a fairly accurate picture of what happened to the competition-winning designs.

In most situations, failures and mistakes are sorted out quietly. Promoters of competitions are not afforded this luxury. Having sought the publicity at the time of the launch, they cannot escape it if things do not then go according to plan. Although competitions do not result in failure as often as the press might suggest, there have been problems over the years. One competition to hit the headlines was for the extension to the National Gallery building in London's Trafalgar Square (1984). It inspired the now famous 'carbuncle' speech, caused great problems for the winning practice and led to the complete revision and redocumentation of the competition system (undertaken jointly by the DoE and RIBA in 1986). Projects which receive most publicity often demonstrate the potential difficulties most effectively.

> Where else but in late twentieth-century Britain could the fiasco of the National
> Gallery extension have taken place? In other capital cities they built competition-
> winning entries – sometimes by British Architects. In London the Houses of
> Parliament and National Gallery extensions and Vauxhall Cross are monuments to
> muddle, vacillation, bad judgement or loss of nerve.
>
> (Editorial in the *Architects' Journal*, April 1985)

What went wrong? The same editorial continues with a search for causes.
'Pathologists now gathering around the corpse will have a field day
identifying the causes of death. Some of these are fairly obvious: the basic
proposition of making the offices subsidise the gallery accommodation
was unsound, the RIBA's wealth of experience in competition administra-
tion was ignored and the original brief was unsatisfactory. In the event it
proved impossible to recover from such fundamental defects.' The assessors could not agree on a winner and were allegedly split on an
architect/trustee basis, eventually agreeing to appoint the architects ABK
provided that they redesigned the scheme and subsequently drew up a
completely new brief. 'What went wrong was that the project was
fundamentally flawed, the brief was inadequate, the promoting body was
not fully committed to the competition process, the rules of the game
were changed as it went along, the architects were excluded from
decisions and others were allowed to lobby for alternative approaches.'
This provides a fair summary of what can go wrong in competitions.

One of the dangers of the competition system is that the process of
selecting the design (i.e. the competition) can become isolated from the
process of getting the project built. A competition is not a self-contained
event starting with an advertisement inviting entries and finishing with
the selection of a winning design. It is a process within a process and can
only succeed if it is seen as an integral and constructive part of a more
extended whole. Planning, consultation and the careful development of a
brief are all essential pre-competition procedures. The promoter needs to
define objectives in terms of what the competition is to achieve and the
contribution it is to make to the overall progress of the project.

Is a competition the best option?

Encouraging more extensive use of the competition system through
funding distribution policies could lead to competitions being promoted
in situations where they are inappropriate or where the promoting body
is antipathetic to the process.

While there is no evidence to suggest that any one type or scale of building, master planning or landscaping project, is incompatible with the competition approach there are situations when a competition may not be the best option. The architectural competition system, even in its more flexible forms, is designed to provide a choice of approaches to a defined set of requirements. Criteria for assessment have to be established. Where these criteria are unclear, where conflicting requirements can only be resolved through negotiation, or where the solutions require a complicated package of different elements to be provided, an architectural competition may prove inappropriate.

In other cases, it is important to match the competition format to the promoter's requirements. A flexible brief only becomes a problem if the competition takes the designs past the stage where change can be made without compromising the design solution. A wide range of selection and briefing procedures is now being used. Each serves a particular purpose. (These procedures are outlined in Chapter 5.)

Before making the decision to promote a competition, the promoter (either as an individual or collectively) needs to gain an understanding of the course on which she or he is proposing to embark. If the responsibility for the eventual commission lies with a board, committee or council, every member of that body needs to accept the rules under which the competition is to operate. Problems occur when individuals seek to change decisions which have been delegated, challenge agreed procedures or withdraw from collective decisions. Having decided on the format and agreed a number of safeguards, the full promoting body has to be prepared to endorse the whole procedure. While embarking on a building project is neither a sport nor a game, most UK managers are sufficiently at ease with sports-based analogies to understand that the pitch has to be well prepared, goalposts cannot be moved, rules have to be followed and the umpire's decision is final. Right from the outset, the promoting body must be determined to see the process through to completion. This level of commitment can only be achieved if everybody has been consulted and brought into the earlier decision-making stages.

Where a promoting body is unwilling to accept the basic competition principles, it could be well-advised to seek an alternative form of selecting a designer. Inserting 'additional safeguards' into the system may merely provide loopholes through which the uncommitted promoter will seek to escape, wasting a considerable amount of time, money and goodwill in the process.

As the whole basis of an architectural competition is the quality of design achieved, the system should not be used where the promoter is either unwilling or unable to allow sufficient time (both during and after the competition) for the design to be developed or to pay adequate fees for the work to be properly carried out.

Establishing the context

Solutions can only be offered when problems have been defined. It is at this stage that some competitions begin to 'go wrong'. The DoE guidelines set the scene: 'Too often basic objectives have not been explored in sufficient depth at the outset; one consequence is that the competition merely exposes uncertainties in the situation or unresolved conflicts within the client body.'

Promoters of successful competitions all emphasise the amount of time and effort which was needed to prepare for the competition. The process of research and testing of proposals cannot be put aside in the hope that the competitors will sort out inherent problems. It has to be carried out far more assiduously than for a project where the architect is appointed to work on the development of the brief.

One architect, with a great deal of experience of the competition system, cited the case where he asked to see the brief before agreeing to act as an assessor for a competition about to be launched by a university authority. The brief was due out the following week but, alarmed by its inconsistencies and lack of real information, he quickly put together a ten page questionnaire. The result was that the competition was postponed, three different committees were formed to look at different aspects of the problem and a new brief was drawn up one year later. (This competition is not the subject of any of the case studies featured in this book.)

Briefing is a specialist skill. Where the promoting body does not have its own technical staff or advisers, it should consider bringing in consultants to work on the brief. The South Bank Board appointed architects DEGW to prepare the brief for its competition (see Case study 9). Their job was to analyse the problems, collect and collate information and present the whole in a form which would enable the competition entrants to work out solutions. These two processes – the briefing and the response – can be seen as separate parts of a single 'dialogue'. Where the problem is complex, there may be advantages to separating the process of identifying problems from that of providing solutions. It could be argued that these processes draw on different sets of skills and that the competition system provides an effective way of securing the best team for each one of them.

Testing the brief

Although competitions can help resolve very difficult issues, they cannot solve impossible problems. A brief needs to be tested to ensure that its basic requirements can be met before competitors are asked to spend time working out design solutions. A brief which is substantially flawed can lead to one of a number of possible outcomes. Some competitors will identify the flaws and decide against entering – leaving the field open to those designers who were either unable to detect the faulty brief or thought it did not matter. Where none of the entries is able to meet the requirements of the brief, selecting a winner could prove exceedingly difficult. If a winning scheme is selected, it is likely that the architect will then have to reopen the whole briefing process and redesign the building – and probably accept much of the blame for the fact that the project takes too long or goes over cost or, in the worst scenario, has to be abandoned.

Some of the problems experienced in the National Gallery competition recurred in the competition to redevelop the Royal Opera House and its surroundings (promoted 1983). Once again the brief asked for a substantial commercial input which would finance the required provision for the arts. The competition was generally considered to have been well run and to have produced a good design by a competent team (Jeremy Dixon in association with Building Design Partnership), who were subsequently commissioned to carry out further studies. Twelve years and some millions of pounds later, they are still working on it.

Some 'flawed brief' problems relate to the site. There have been examples of competitions where the required accommodation could not be fitted on the site; where the site was incorrectly shown and not properly delineated; where the site or part of it could not be used (ancient burial grounds put an end to one competition and resulted in another only being partially completed); where the designated site could not be acquired or where it required special foundations which resulted in the winning scheme going way over budget. In one case, the site was lost to a higher bidder half way through the competition. The whole project had to be abandoned and the prize money was shared out amongst the first-stage winners.

Some competitions failed because the promoters got their costing wrong. There have been examples of projects where the brief could not possibly have been met within the allocated budget, however skilled the designer. The Museum of Scotland Trustees took the precaution of commissioning an outline design to determine the cost before securing the funding. (The process was also used to check that the required accommodation could be fitted onto a tight city-centre site.) While this might seem an expensive process, it achieved its objective and may well have resulted in savings in the longer term (see Case study 3).

Where all the shortlisted schemes come in over budget, the reason could be that the cost limits were set too low for the scale and quality of provision required. If the project is to proceed, the promoter could be well advised to rethink this aspect before requiring cutbacks to be made. Where cost is a crucial factor, it could be worth considering the procedure used by the National Trust in its Langdon Cliffs competition. The Trust appointed (and paid) its own cost advisers to be available to each of the shortlisted competitors so that their schemes could be tested against stringent financial objectives at an early stage (see Case study 6). The advantage of this method is that all competitors are working to the same cost assessment procedures.

Other schemes have failed because the promoters were over-optimistic about their fundraising abilities. While the system is sometimes used to give a boost to fundraising or to show good intent to potential funding bodies, it does not lend itself to projects of a purely speculative nature. Competitions run as kite flying exercises do not have a good record. There is too much scope for circumstances and requirements to change between the design and eventual implementation of the protect.

The responsibility for things going wrong does not always lie with the promoter. Good designers are not necessarily easy to work with. One project failed to materialise because the winning architects refused to adapt their design when it was shown to be over budget. When the architect assessor was next asked to advise on a competition he recommended the promoters to interview all the shortlisted competitors to check that they were prepared to be adaptable (although this was not made explicit at the time). Where a competition does not involve any element of pre-selection, the promoter choice system can provide a safeguard. Some 'difficult' architects can produce very good buildings but only when they are working in association with a promoter who is able to accommodate their particular style and approach.

Quantity surveyors can err on the side of generosity when it comes to assessing what can be built within the competition cost target. The cost assessments of the competitors' consultants and those of the promoter's consultants can vary considerably. (A 10% discrepancy is not generally regarded as being out of line.) Where cost is an important factor, a financial adviser needs to be appointed early in the process to work out ways of detailing the cost elements and to establish the basis on which these are to be calculated.

It is perhaps salutory to recall that none of the three competitions promoted by architectural organisations (one by the RIBA, 1986, and two by the Architects' Benevolent Society, during the 1970s) resulted in a building. One encountered problems because a large section of the site proved unusable, the second was under-budgeted and the third asked for designs for a scheme where there was virtually no chance of the necessary funding becoming available.

Consultation

There are various ways of working to ensure that a competition proceeds though all its stages and results in a completed building. The one that is allegedly used for some of the 'grand projets' in France, is where the promoter takes the decision to build and then just presses forward. President Pompidou was said to have held regular meetings with the young Richard Rogers in order to smooth the way for the then outrageously different Arts Centre to be built. Another method, perhaps more suitable for this country, is to gather as wide a base of support as possible and then negotiate any hurdles which stand in the way.

Many competition projects are intrinsically controversial – often they are for significant 'one-off' buildings on strategic sites with a wide and varied constituency of special interests. If the individuals and groups which represent these interests are not brought into the consultation process and their views are not duly recognised in the briefing for the competition, they are unlikely to be satisfied with the outcome. There are a number of competitions where the winning schemes have failed because they did not prove acceptable to other interest groups. This was one of the causes of the problems which beset the Cardiff Bay Opera House Trust competition (1995) and nearly unsettled the result.

The Cardiff Bay competition also demonstrated that public consultation has to be geared to the stage the competition has reached. The result was generally considered to be a controversial one – both in terms of the architect selected and the style of her winning design. The debate rapidly focussed not on the quality of the scheme but on whether or not it was acceptable to the general public. John Redwood, the then Secretary of State for Wales, stepped in with the statement, 'It is important that this has the goodwill of the people of Wales. If they vote strongly against the design, I hope the trustees take that into account and change it.' Francis Duffy, President of the RIBA, took this point up in a letter to *The Independent* (December 1994):

> Suddenly, cynically, after all the hard work and careful assessment, public opinion is now evoked. There is a role for public participation in lottery projects – but at the time when decisions on the building brief are made. To pretend that real public consultation can take place after a design competition has been run and won is nonsense.

Once the competition has been assessed and the result announced, consultation processes need to focus on the development and implementation of the winning design.

It is not only promoters of national projects who can find controversy difficult to handle. For example, one developer promoted a competition to secure a good design for a sensitive city-centre site. He was pleased with the result but local opinion, spearheaded by the local paper, wanted a more traditional approach. The winning design was never built. Its architects put the failure down to the fact that the promoter was a sociable man who 'just got fed up with being ostracised at the golf club'. Wider consultation before the brief was drawn up (as well as a bit of strategic planning before the result was announced) could well have helped the situation.

The competition system offers more scope for consultation than is generally used, although the promoters of more successful competitions are picking up this aspect. The case studies demonstrate a whole variety of procedures, pre-briefing discussion seminars, explanatory publications and exhibitions, artists' forums, schools' workshops, input from user groups and neighbours, discussion documents and attitude surveys.

The competition for the new college at Durham University began with a series of artists' forums at which artists and designers discussed criteria for the development of the site (see Case study 8).

The Trustees of the Museum of Scotland held a seminar to launch their competition for a new building at which the whole process was explained. The proceedings were then published (see Case study 3).

The South Downs Health NHS Trust mounted a small competition for the design of a clinic which was such a success that they decided to use the system again for a larger scheme (see Case study 7). It involved bringing in a 'user group' panel of community nurses, health visitors, GPs and local councillors and exhibiting the six entries where anyone with a particular interest could look and comment. Their observations were passed on to the assessors. The promoter comments: 'A major advantage of this method was the enthusiasm and involvement of staff at all levels, who felt that not only were their ideas listened to, but they actually influenced the choice of design solution.'

Another promoter, though enthusiatic about the result of the competition and about the effective interaction amongst the many different interest groups, warned of one danger inherent in the process. 'If people are asked to comment, they then think that everything they say will be in the resulting project. Sometimes this just isn't possible to achieve.' The competition procedure needs to be carefully explained so that everybody understands how it works and accepts the compromises required in the interests of achieving the best possible solution in the given circumstances.

Planning interests

An issue which requires careful handling is that of planning. The way the planning system operates in this country is that detailed planning consent is directly linked to a particular scheme. A competition winner, once appointed, has both the obligation and the right to open negotiations with the relevant planning authority. While planning cannot be secured in advance by following a set of conditions, it does not mean that planning requirements can be ignored until the competition is won. Some planning officers claim that competitions try to 'set their own agendas'.

Various systems have been used to integrate planning requirements into the competition briefing process. One method is to provide 'context' information as part of the brief, that is documents which set out the background against which the project is to be developed. These could comprise a series of papers written by a number of sectional interest groups or could be based on an early discussion seminar. Sometimes the question and answer procedures take the form of a seminar to which the planning officer is invited, together with other consultants. Planning officers can be asked to join a team of technical advisers or to comment (but not recommend or exclude on planning grounds) during the various stages of the competition.

Differences and disagreements

Some promoters complain that competitors are not sufficiently realistic when designs are being produced for a competition entry. One promoter writes: 'Because competitions require unpaid effort (usually) there seems to be a gap between what can be designed to win a competition and what is likely to be built afterwards.' A number of promoters have experienced problems in implementing competition-winning schemes. Some of them occur because the brief was ill-thought but, in the main, the problems relate to what competitors describe as 'rewriting the brief' and promoters call 'adapting to changed circumstances'. One competition promoter observed:

> When coming to re-cost the winning design, it was found to be much more expensive than originally envisaged. We discussed the possibility of a reduced scheme, but the winning architects were unwilling to compromise their original design.

Whether or not the relationship survives, depends to a certain extent on how each partner judges the other's motives. What one may see as a request for flexibility, the other may regard as pressure to compromise the design quality which won the competition. All competitions depend on a certain degree of flexibility being shown on all sides. Things only 'go wrong' when one or other of the participants refuses to accommodate the others. Many people consider that face to face interviews during the competition help the promoter and architects to understand each other's problems and prepare the foundations for a good working relationship. Increasingly, the design work in a competition is being limited to a 'design approach' (particularly in the first stage of a two-stage competition) and flexibility is established as a key criteria in the brief.

There may also be disagreements amongst different members of the panel of assessors. Although split juries do occur, they are much rarer than the debate on competitions may suggest. The RIBA's recommendation that the jury be kept small makes factions more difficult to establish and in most cases the result appears to be reached amicably and with a considerable degree of unanimity. Occasionally a jury split results in a compromise being reached which excludes all the first choices in favour of a less controversial second choice. This could cause difficulties when the result is announced, especially if a high quality but potentially controversial design is passed over in favour of an obviously 'safe' option. The widespread use of the promoter choice system makes the promoter/architect jury division an increasingly rare event.

Any procedure which results in one person or group being preferred to another can cause contention. Competitions are no exception. Like any other group, architects have an effective network of communication – it deals equally in information and in rumour. If a competition decision is considered in any way 'suspect', stories of how it came to be made will be spread and reinvented. This means that disputes need careful handling. Problems which are swept under the carpet are unlikely to remain there for very long.

Handling the announcement

Each stage of the building process needs to be anticipated and planned well in advance. Just as the necessary research and consultation procedures have to be put in hand well before the competition is launched, the promoter needs a strategy to handle the outcome of the competition and secure the appointment of the winning architect. Some promoters appear to be taken by surprise when the selection process is complete and only then start thinking about what they are going to do next. As a general principle, the promoter needs to plan his or her response and make sure of the support for the winning scheme within his or her own organisation and from those with a particular interest in the project before it is thrown into the arena of public debate.

Firstly, the promoting body has to be properly briefed. John Spencely warned the Museum of Scotland Trustees at the launch of the competition: 'Everybody will care passionately about the process and the result can only be decided by the exercise of collective judgement. Everybody is going to have their own views on whether the winner is a worthy winner or not.' The merits of the selected scheme and the basis on which it was selected need to be explained to members of the promoting body before any public announcement is made. If the result is likely to be a controversial one, the announcement needs to be handled as a public relations exercise and designed to secure support.

Where the promoter's commitment is seen to be anything less than total, it gives a signal to the losing competitors that the field is still open – with the result that the winning scheme comes under attack from all sides.

The National Trust was faced with what it knew to be a potentially difficult planning application and had the foresight to make plans to block any lobby which might develop for alternative schemes. The competition conditions not only forbad any circulation of competition designs before the result was announced but made the competitors' honoraria dependent on this embargo being observed. The Trust proceeded to negotiate planning permission on the winning design and, once this was secured, announced the result (see Case study 6). This could provide a useful format for other promoters who want to control the announcement of the result. (The Trust had been taken care to consult widely at the briefing stage and to draw key interests into the assessment process so it could not be said that it imposed a winner on an unprepared public.)

Once the promoter has prepared the ground, exhibitions can be mounted and meetings organised. As the final decision has already been made, the presentation needs to focus attention on the qualities of the winning design and involve the winning architects. Where the competition is for an approach rather than a fully worked out building, a further programme of consultation could be appropriate (see Case study 9: The South Bank Centre). If properly managed, public interest can help to carry the scheme forward.

Arbitration and dispute

Competitions are a form of contract. The promoter produces a set of documents setting out the rules and requirements. Competitors respond by submitting designs in accordance with these rules and requirements and in doing so accept the terms on which the contract is offered.

Most competition rules include a clause to cover disputes. The RIBA guidelines suggest the following clause be included in the conditions: 'In the event of any dispute between the parties prior to the signature of the agreement as to its terms and conditions, the matter shall be referred to the assessors whose decision shall be final.' There have been occasions when the assessors have intervened and succeeded in reaching an agreed settlement.

Independently run competitions tend to reserve all rights of settlement to the promoting body. For example, 'The decisions of the Trustees of the Tate Gallery in all matters relating to this competition will be final.' As disputes tend to be between competitors and the promoter, a clause worded in this way acts more as an attempt at embargo than as a prospective means of conciliation. This is one of the problems of an unregulated competition system – there is no intermediary court of appeal if disputes arise.

There are two areas which give rise to dispute: the payment of the design fees due as a result of the competition and design copyright. One problem which has arisen in the past is where the promoter requires additional work before agreeing to an appointment. This work has to be financed by the architect. If the appointment is then delayed or fails to be made, the architect will seek payment for fees due. In one recent case the architect was forced to sue the promoter before an out of court settlement was agreed in his favour. The question of copyright is also becoming more of an issue as the demand for competitive work increases. Clients ask for a number of design solutions and then pick the ideas which they consider suit them best. This is not always as cynical and calculated as it appears. Some inexperienced clients genuinely believe that this is how the system works – until they are threatened with legal action.

7 Working through competition

The media-led competitions debate tends to skirt round the fact that current practice in this country requires a very significant proportion of all new commissions to be bid for in some way and that many of these bids involve design work.

This was one of the subjects which was discussed with architects when researching for this book. One large London based practice stated that virtually 100% of its work had to be gained in this way. Even their previous clients required them to bid against other equally known and established architects, on a shortlist of four or so. This particular architectural practice is broadly based but gains a significant amount of its work from large commercial or publicly funded bodies with continuing commissioning programmes. Some smaller practices specialising in working for individual clients were able to find work in less competitive situations. An arts and conservation based practice, for instance, secured virtually all of its increasing workload through existing clients and recommendations, although it had not always been in this position. These are extremes. All practices are affected to some extent and have had to adapt their working methods accordingly.

Although the increasing workload may mitigate the impact of competitive work, all the indications are that the bid system, in some form or other, is here to stay. The fee scale, in its old mandatory form, is almost certainly a thing of the past. The Monopolies Commission and the Office of Fair Trading keep a watchful eye on any form of professional cabal and EC legislation endorses the concept of selection through competition as one of its key elements. This leaves the problem in the hands of the individual architect and the individual practice. To function in a changed and still changing environment they have no option but to accommodate and, where possible, to discriminate.

Counting the cost

Any form of bidding for a commission which involves designs or design approaches being prepared in competition with others places additional expense on every day practice. One large firm of architects, which gains much of its work in this way estimated that the bids which included a design element had cost them between £2 000 and £100 000 to prepare. The low figure represented the cost of preparing a submission including a 'design approach' in response to a fairly standard outline brief for a commercial (office based) development – an area in which the practice had considerable experience. The top figure was a 'one-off' submission for an international competition which had the potential to introduce the practice to a range of interesting and financially rewarding new commissions.

The senior partner of another established practice wrote: 'A high proportion of our work is the subject of competition. The nature of the information required varies from simple feasibility studies for small sites to complex bids involving housing associations, contractor developers and other professionals including those in the economic and social fields.' Examples of typical figures covering competition entries over the last three years showed costs in a similar range to those quoted above (see Table 7.1).

Table 7.1 *Project costs and fee income*

Project	Date	Value	Potential fee income	Cost to practice
Urban regeneration	1993/4	£100 m	£4 m	£116 000
City centre redevelopment	1993/4	£4 m	£300 000	£12 000
Urban regeneration	1994	£80 m	£3.2 m	£45 000
Health care building	1994	£2.7 m	£160 000	£12 000
Commercial office building	1994	£1.35 m	£50 000	£5 000
Urban housing	1993	£15 m	£380 000	£24 000
Urban housing and facilities	1994	£66 m	£750 000	£84 000
Commercial office building	1993	£1.7 m	£100 000	£8 000

Analysing the return

The other crucial figure which a practice needs to take into account when working out the costs and benefits of competitive work is the possible 'hit rate'. How often can a practice expect to win? Figures published in the *RIBA*

Table 7.2 *Competition hit list: how many, how often, how much? (This information is reproduced with permission of the* RIBA **Journal.***)*

Foster
- Entered 49 competitions in past five years
- Not known how many are open/invited/ seeded
- Five UK competitions, 44 foreign
- Won eight, lost 34, decisions outstanding on seven
- Success rate: 19%

Rogers
- Entered 47 competitions in past five years
- Of these, 14 were open and 33 invited
- 35 were foreign and 12 UK
- Won 18, came second or third in four, 25 either lost or awaiting result
- Success rate: 38%

Future Systems
- Entered 12 competitions in past five years
- Seven invited, five open
- Five UK, seven foreign
- Won two, second three, unplaced seven
- 'Impossibleto say how much we spend but a lot!'
- Success rate: 17%

Cullinan
- Entered 11 competitions in past five years
- Eight invited and three open competitions
- 10 UK and one foreign
- Won four and lost seven
- Practice reckons to spend about 600–700 hours per competition
- Success rate: 36%

Matthew Priestman
- Entered 12 competitions in past five years
- Nine open, one invited, two seeded
- Six UK and six foreign
- Won two, lost 10
- Spends about £12 000 a year on competitions
- Success rate: 17%

Journal show success rates varying between 17% and 38% but a glance at the practices involved will show that these figures are unlikely to reflect the experience of the average UK-based practice (Table 7.2).

One large practice not listed here gave its success rate as 10% but rapidly acknowledged that it regarded the figure as unacceptable and was looking for ways to improve the situation. Occasionally firms have a run of luck – or inspiration. Architects Pardey and Yee, who describe themselves as 'products of the competition system', were featured in the *Architects' Journal* (January 1990) as having achieved a 50% win record. They had entered six competitions, won three and were runners-up in the other three, all within a year. The now well-established practice of Allies and Morrison was also developed through a series of competition wins. It can claim a success rate of 25% over the last decade. (They entered 28, won seven, were second in eight and amongst the finalists in most of the others.) These costs and hit rates generally relate to a 'package' of competitions including the invited shortlist and the large scale open international format.

In the past, entering a competition was often regarded as a design exercise – a welcome break from routine and a bit of stimulation for the office. It was not seen as part of the everyday process of securing a commission. This has changed. Bidding for work on a competitive design basis can mean that a practice has to invest anything up to 10% of the potential fee income for each bid made. In this climate, assessing which competition to enter and working out how much time is to be spent on preparing the submission becomes a crucial commercial decision. Practices have to judge what return they can expect and make decisions accordingly. The cost figures set out in Table 7.1 give one example of how this operates. Where substantial costs were incurred, they relate to bids for new areas of work. The potential return (i.e. the fee income proportional to the cost of the competitive design work) increases when the practice is working in an area in which it already has experience. These regular and recurring figures represent the cost of getting work through competition.

The reason architects enter competitions is that they want the commission. On this basis any cost benefit is a straight calculation of money invested against fee income earned over a given period of time. There are, however, other gains to be made from entering competitions which, in industrial or commercial terms, fall into the categories of marketing and product development. In marketing terms, the aim is to publicise the skills of the practice and to make contact with new clients. Not all competitions provide the same opportunities. Many competitive procedures are so closed that the only people who know anything about them are the client and the few practices invited to take part. The ones which are likely to be picked up by both press and other potential clients are open competitions (with a preliminary trawl at the very least) or those for high profile projects. Gaining work through the publicity attached to competitions is very much a hit and miss affair but it does appear to work to a practice's advantage over a period of time. The competition conditions should indicate whether or not a particular promoter is going to mount an exhibition and what proportion of the entries he or she intends to show. There are competitions which are promoted as public events – either to raise the profile and attract funding for a project or to demonstrate 'best endeavour'. Others leave it entirely to the competitors to take advantage of opportunities provided by the competition.

Looked at in terms of product development, competitions provide an opportunity for architects to research and gain expertise in different areas.

For this to be of value, the competition needs to be one in which there is a well-thought out brief; where the assessors are qualified and respected in their fields; where the entries are properly assessed and analysed (with full circulation of the assessors' report); and where an exhibition is held so that comparisons of approach can be made.

Organising the practice

As entering competitions becomes an integral part of practice, architects are reassessing their working methods.

A consultant to one large practice drew up guidelines to be followed whenever some form of competition was required:

> With the bigger practice, there appeared to be a greater capacity for time to be wasted through not having an agreed procedure. Decisions were ad-hoc and the wheel was repeatedly being re-invented. . . . Many of the points may well appear self-evident, even obvious. Astonishingly, however, so many of them seemed frequently to be ignored.

His guidelines covered appointing a design team leader with the necessary support staff, establishing a broad programme, identifying the key requirements in the brief and working out what specialist skills would be required, setting objectives, clarifying lines of decision making and refining presentation methods.

If competition is the norm, practices need to establish working methods which ensure a balance between input and anticipated return and to concentrate on streamlining procedures as much as is practicable. Many competitions start with the 'initial trawl' and then select people to compete on the basis of expertise and experience. In these situations the first approach can often be covered by the practice brochure, designed to a format which is easily adapted to respond to different competition requirements.

Checking the market

Many architects claim that they are having to operate in a market which makes commercial judgement difficult if not impossible.

Reports of competition malpractice abound. Much of the information comes through the architectural grapevine and is extremely difficult to check. Promoters and assessors do not admit publicly to incompetence, lack of authority, devious practices or manipulation. The experiences which are reported, however, are sufficiently corroborative for some conclusions to be drawn.

Competitions are held which ask for a substantial input of design work and then assess on the basis of the lowest fee bid. There are some promoters who do not appear to know what they want and think that the way to find out is to ask a lot of different architects to research the problem and provide design solutions. In some cases, they take these solutions and, instead of appointing the architects responsible, find alternative (cheaper) ways of proceeding. There are promoters who ask far more people to prepare detailed design work than they need for a choice of approach and then do not take the trouble to either stage the competition or to draw up a shortlist of entrants. Others do not bother to specify or restrict the scale and amount of material to be submitted with the result that the largest practice sets the level and the smaller ones struggle to match it. One architect comments: 'We have on occasions had to press promoters or try to reach informal agreements with fellow competitors to limit the amount of work. It really should be set out and enforced by the promoter.' In many competitions the only reward is the job and in some of these the winners find that even this is offered at a substantially reduced fee rate. All other design work is seen as one of the perks of the process. Sometimes the result is quietly set aside. In one recent competition, the only communication the winning architects received from the local authority promoter was a Christmas card.

Invited competitions can cause dilemmas. Practices which have already been working for a particular client feel they cannot turn down an invitation to compete, whatever the basis of the competition. High profile clients and those which have a continuing flow of work to offer are in a powerful position. Some appear to take advantage of this.

One architect who has been able to maintain a good record of competition successes still comments: 'Our experience with competitions has often been less than satisfactory . . . whether architects are to blame for their innocence or the organisers for their behaviour, the situation is often iniquitous and clearly in need of reform.'

The recession trapped architects into taking any and all opportunities to gain work on whatever basis it was offered. Current indications are that the construction industry is on a continuing if somewhat slow upturn. This should restore some element of choice. If the 'iniquitous situation' which so many architects claim to experience in competitions is to improve, they need to exercise choice as soon as it becomes an option and to discriminate effectively between good and bad competition prospects.

The basic principles of the competition system, set out in Chapter 5 primarily as a guide for potential promoters, should be well known to architects. They have been developed over the whole of the last century and are followed by official competition systems throughout the world. Until architects begin to turn down invitations for excessive, ill-rewarded or unregulated competitive work – and explain their reasons for doing so –

clients who believe there are advantages to playing the system in this way will continue to do so.

A university invited ten practices to submit designs for a new £3.5 million development. Four of them withdrew after discovering that the promoter intended to retain the copyright of the three winning schemes. One of those who declined to take part also commented on the poorly written brief, the excessive design input required and the lack of time and opportunity for consultation. The university, however, expressed itself to be satisfied with the competition on the basis that there were still six firms who were prepared to compete. (This information is taken from a report which appeared in *Building Design*, April 1994.)

Senior members of the profession could take a lead. High profile architects are, on occasions, asked to act as assessors because their names give credence to the project. In market terms they are being used as a form of product endorsement. If they allow themselves to become involved in competition projects which do not follow established good practice procedures, they endorse the methods used and make them appear acceptable to others. One architect who was questioned about his role as an assessor in a major competition, said that he was 'uncomfortable' with the conditions. (This was reported in an article on competitions entitled 'Exploitation's willing hands', *Building Design*, January 1994.) The competition – organised by a national institution – went ahead as planned.

Assessing the competition options

Although the current situation is a difficult one, it is worth spending some time trying to 'spot the duds' and to work out what the potential gains might be from any particular competition. 'Qualifying the prospect' is a term used in marketing/sales in the commercial and business sector. It involves making assessments of opportunities so that the time and money available can be directed towards those areas which show most potential.

The format architects look for, when considering competitive opportunities, is one where there are fewer than six or so entries, the amount of work required is limited and clearly stated, the selection criteria are established at the outset. Some architects recommend that a colloquium is held beforehand to enable all competitors to raise questions prior to starting work. This is seen as being of great value to both the competitors and to promoters in ensuring that the submissions reflect the promoter's needs. They also require a firm commitment to build or for the winner to be compensated if no commission results from the competition. Anything less amounts to a double gamble, i.e. if there is only a 50% chance of a commission for the winning architect the original odds are lengthened substantially. The system of negotiated fees is now generally accepted provided it is separated from the design assessment. Good practice requires that a sum of money is paid to each competitor for their efforts – both to reimburse the architects for some of the cost involved and to demonstrate the promoter's good intent.

Given the choice, many established practices would limit their regular competitive work to this type of competition, entering the occasional open competition to develop skills and extend opportunities into new areas. At the moment the choice is a more complicated one. For many architects it has to be a case of avoiding the worst rather than picking the best.

Assess the background

One of the first questions to be considered is why the competition is being held. The standard reply is 'to secure a design of the highest quality' but the underlying reasons, if they can be discovered, give more indication of whether or not the competition is likely to result in a commission for the winning architect. Some promoters use the system purely as a public relations exercise. Festivals and conferences have a bad record as far as competitions are concerned. Where a competition is launched as part of a national or international event it can get forgotten once the event has finished. One example which hit the headlines was Alsop and Stormer's competition-winning design for Swansea's National Centre for Literature. After winning with a design for a £12.5 million new building for the City of Literature 1995, Alsop and Stormer were first asked to draw up a much smaller new building and then look at a possible conversion. The promoter subsequently went ahead with a design and build refurbishment scheme involving local architects.

The winning architect of another well publicised set of competitions claimed that, 'the council never intended nor did it have the will to build the scheme. We felt the whole thing was a vehicle for the council's promotion and that the competitions were a sideshow.'

Fundraising exercises also have a mixed record. The Dulwich Picture Gallery competition, for example, attracted record levels of interest and a considerable amount of publicity but the winning design still remains an idea on the drawing board. Housing association work is a recognised problem area in that funding can only be secured on the basis of an approved design – so designs have to be secured without payment. Winning a competition in this area does not carry with it any guarantees of favourable consideration. This could also prove to be a stumbling block with some lottery projects.

Disagreements within the promoting body spell problems for a competition winner. There are several examples of competition schemes which have floundered because the winning scheme did not succeed in uniting support or because an opposing group got into a stronger position. Many architects have fallen victim to high profile projects which are put out to competition because promoters knew they would prove contentious.

The problem with a competition which fails to result in a built project is that the winning architect is unlikely to be paid for the work done. (The first prize is only an advance of fees due.) The competition process should be seen as one which continues right through to the appointment of the winning architect. The fees for the design work done in the competition then become payable. In practice many promoters, including some who have taken the trouble to follow RIBA or RIAS procedures, consider the competition as being at an end when the result is announced. There are situations where, regardless of any offers made, there is no additional money available (e.g. where the prizes were sponsored in advance of a fundraising campaign). In others, the promoters avoid taking the decision to abandon the competition by just letting things drift. While this may cause frustration, the situation which gives rise to most resentment is where the promoter asks for further work to be carried out before any formal appointment is made – and then abandons the project. Getting payment for work done in this way can prove very difficult.

Competition conditions, even where one of the professional institutes are involved, need to be read carefully. One winning competitor outlines his position:

> The competition itself was set up by the RIAS in association with the client, stating a 'firm intention to engage the winning practice' at the outset. Now six months on from the awards of the competition we have received only one communication from the client stating that they cannot guarantee a commission since they may form a partnership with a developer having their own consultants.

Intentions can always be changed. What is needed is a commitment to appoint. This does not guarantee that the architect will get the job but it does mean that they have the right to claim payment for the design work done in the course of the competition.

Some architects look to the professional institutes to 'do something' about competition payments and fees. As things stand at present, the institutes have sufficient problems in persuading would-be promoters to accept the much modified conditions under which their current systems operate. Their ability to require or enfore additional commitments is very limited. It rests with individual architects either to avoid 'insecure' competitions, enlist the support of co-competitors in trying to improve what is on offer, seek to procure commitments through careful use of any question and answer procedures which may exist, ask for help from any independent assessors, use procrastination techniques to avoid additional work prior to appointment and/or threaten legal action when published rules are not properly observed.

Judge the promoter's intent

The official competition systems aim to provide a number of safeguards and the fact that a promoter is prepared to work through a professional body demonstrates a level of impartiality and commitment to good practice procedures. The RIBA and RIAS take some responsibility for assessing a promoter's intent. When rules are broken in competitions which they manage or endorse, it becomes their responsibility to sort things out. There are examples of these organisations negotiating between the promoter and winning team – often using the 'good offices' of the senior architect assessor for the project.

Only a very small proportion of competitions are organised by the professional institutes. With all the others, intending competitors have to make their own judgements. Recent competition history suggests that the status of an organisation does not provide an adequate basis for assessing the integrity of the competition it promotes. The ethics of the market economy require that those in the most powerful position demand the best deal. Competitions promoted by organisations or individuals within them who subscribe to these ethics will most probably seek to secure 'the most for the least', especially when they are operating on a 'one-off' basis. Promoters who commission regularly are more likely to understand the design process and apply some quality based value for money criteria. Where a promoter (whether an organisation or an individual) sees its role as patron rather than purchaser, the competition rules are more likely to be directed towards securing the best design and may well be more generous to the architect. The most reliable guide is the promoter's own record.

Some assessment of intent can be gained from a careful reading of the conditions. The composition and status of the jury is one indicator (see below). Prize money is also important as it demonstrates that the promoter appreciates the design effort involved and is willing to make a financial investment to balance that required of the competitors. In some cases there are other factors at work which place limitations on what can be offered (e.g. government spending controls). A better indicator than 'total size of prize fund' could be the relationship between the prize money offered and the amount of work required. The other key area to look at is the commitment to appoint the winner. Once again there may be factors which prevent the promoter making a firm commitment to appoint the architect and proceed with the building (e.g. funding). But it is worth assessing what commitment a promoter could make and comparing it with that set out in the conditions. If the commitment is a weak one, some balancing recompense may be offered.

There are promoters who claim to be following RIBA or RIAS guidelines but give various reasons for not seeking 'official' endorsement. Most independently run competitions, however closely they appear to follow

RIBA formats, change two important clauses. One is the commitment to appoint the winning architect and the other relates to the settlement of disputes.

Assess the assessors

The choice of assessors and the way the jury is constituted can tell competitors quite a lot about a competition. Some commentators claim that by selecting the assessors, the promoter selects the winning design (i.e. style dictates style). This is debatable in all but the most obvious cases. The composition of the jury will however often give a guide to the promoter's main areas of concern. If design is to be the key criteria, this is likely to be reflected in the composition of the jury. Where the jury comprises mainly board members and their employees with no or limited design experience, it could indicate that other criteria are being applied. Competitors may then decide to adapt their entries accordingly. Sometimes juries are given advisory status with the promoter reserving the right to overrule any decisions they reach. In such a situation, competitors could draw the conclusion that the promoter fears a controversial result or an inexperienced or too innovative winner.

In many cases the assessors are asked to select two or three equal winners (promoter choice system) for consideration by the promoter. Competitors could gamble on a 'safe' design being the eventual preferred option. Although many architects suspect that the promoter choice system works in this way, it remains a gamble. There is no evidence to support the suspicion. Where a representative of the promoting organisation has been fully involved in the assessment process, they may well come to share a jury's enthusiasm for a more innovative project and then be in a position to convince colleagues of its merits.

Assessing competitions requires a particular set of skills. Good assessors have to be able to recognise the merits of a variety of different approaches. Big names do not ensure sensitivity of approach, open minded judgement, professional generosity, willingness to give time to ensuring the best outcome or a commitment to the principles of the competition system. Assessors, like promoters, have to be judged on their record.

Assess the brief

The quality of the brief gives a good indication of the quality of the competition. A well-researched and carefully drawn up brief reflects a serious and professional approach to the whole process. It is not a question of detail but of effectively communicating the key requirements. Where the brief is muddled, it is likely to reflect the muddled thinking of the promoter. If they have not set the parameters or identified the problems adequately, there is a strong chance that the solutions prepared by the competitors will not provide the answers the promoter requires. In some cases, promoters only find out what they want through the work done in a competition. Having used the competition to research the brief, they then look for cheaper or easier methods of development:

> When the result was announced the . . . officials then tried to renegotiate the terms of the competition. All they wanted the winner to do was simply revise the design in accordance with a new brief they had prepared as a result of the competition. They then wanted to take over all of the working drawings and supervision of the contract.

Assess the submission requirements

A well-run competition selects from the available procedures those best suited to its needs. Good practice requires that the promoter only asks for design work sufficient to his or her purpose. Whether or not a promoter has these concerns can be deduced from looking at the selection and pre-selection systems used and by the submission requirements at each stage. There could be a number of reasons for a promoter making excessive demands on competitors. Often it is an attempt by inexperienced managers to impress superiors (or funding bodies) with the thoroughness of the selection process. In some cases promoters are advised (or ill-advised) by consultants that such procedures are the accepted way of operating. Some architects will have enough confidence in their own skills to go along with the situation believing that, should they win the commission, they will then be in a position to steer the client down a more productive route. Others may doubt the wisdom of embarking on the project. While in many cases the mismatch between what is demanded and what is needed will not be an extreme one, this relationship is worth considering when an assessment of a competition is being made.

Improving the odds

Practices with some success in competitions are loath to offer advice as to how it is done – partly because they are aware that there are no guarantees to success. One good year could easily be followed by a bad one. Some principles, however, emerge from a study of a range of competitions over a number of years.

Getting on the shortlist

Many competitions now start with an initial trawl of interest. (In certain circumstances this is a required by EC directives.) Sometimes the promoter states his criteria for shortlisting clearly in the advertisement. In other cases, the wording is more ambiguous, possibly for fear of 'discriminating' in terms of the EC requirements. In most cases the promoter will be looking for evidence of ability both to design and implement the project so experience in both building type and scale will be a pre-requisite for selection. Style may also be important but could work in both ways. A promoter may be shortlisting to give a range of approaches or picking the 'best' of a given style of approach.

Some promoters ask for a report or outline approach at this stage. Subsequent shortlisting in some recent competitions suggests that these do not play a significant part in the selection process (i.e. although they may be used to choose between equals they will not get a competitor on to a shortlist unless already picked out on the basis of other – possibly unstated – requirements).

Catching the assessors' attention

'Keep it simple' is the advice given by one competition winner. Another successful competition based practice picks up this theme with the comment, 'In most competitions it is a case of getting across the main idea – possibly developing one or two subsiduary ideas at the most. Some architects think that a competition has to contain their life history.' In open competitions, particularly, the basic approach has to be one which readily attracts the assessors' interest. The detail only becomes relevant once the scheme has got through the initial shortlisting processes. An example which is often cited is the competition drawing 'View to ride' entered in the first stage of the Burrell Gallery competition which showed a window set against a background of trees. This illustrated the competitor's key approach – to set the museum on the edge of the site against existing woodland taking advantage of a setting which complemented the exhibits and provided a natural filter for sunlight. It is said to have taken the competitor through to the second stage when the design team was able to develop the scheme and go on to win the competition.

If the overall approach is not sufficiently persuasive to capture the interest of the assessors, the rest of the work could well be wasted. In the Durham University competition (see Case study 8), John Partridge, the senior architectural assessor describes the judging process:

> The assessors were determined to ask only for a minimum amount in Stage One. In assessing the entries we concentrated on the use of the site and relationship to the City of Durham and the character and philosophy of the approach. We selected six schemes which we felt could develop in their own way.

Similarly the assessors in another competition selected six entries to go through to the second stage, 'where potentially the building would fit well into the context . . . one of the finalists' entries was fairly thoroughly worked out, two were rather less so, and three were definitely sketchy but were included for their potential and because of our appreciation of the general concept'. The Baltic Flour Mill competition aimed to select an architect/ designer to convert the building for installation art. At the RIBA meeting 'Four routes to success' (October 1994) architect assessor Keith Williams described the jury's approach:

> We tried to avoid pre-conceptions, to make a mental blank sheet on design approach. We saw a need to select the designer who showed the most intelligent approach. We looked for sensitivity – the ability to organise a large building in a simple manner and embrace the concept of installation art. We were interested in structure (the building was a large open space with a series of cross walks and lifts). The solution required a structural process which could unstitch the complicated bracing and introduce gallery spaces.

Increasingly, competitions are concentrating on design approaches particularly in the first stage. Assessors say they are looking for evidence of 'quality of thought'. They also try to select schemes which provide alternative approaches for further development when assessing the first stage.

Reading the brief

The competition system works on the basis that designs are assessed against the criteria set out in the brief. The winning design is the one which most successfully fulfils these criteria. A good brief will make its requirements clear. Where this is the case, careful reading and adherence to the details is a pre-requisite to success in the competition.

Competition briefs come in many forms – some better than others. While designs which flout the basic requirements will normally be rejected by the jury, the fine print is sometimes more difficult to interpret. If it proves impossible to meet all the given criteria, competitors may need to assess which ones are the most important for the particular promoter. One practice with a good competition record admitted they can sometimes misread a competition brief: 'We got it wrong on day one and spent the rest of our time embroidering the mistake.' Another young team, disappointed after a winning run, tried to explain their subsequent lack of success: 'We failed to read between the lines of briefs that called for innovation but really required commercial solutions.' Reading between the lines should not be necessary – a good brief makes its requirements clear while a mediocre brief is likely to mislead between the lines as well as on them. What may happen in competitions which ask for innovation and then select what is regarded as a more run of the mill solution is that the quality of entries forced a compromise on the jury. One assessor, disappointed by the quality of entries in a competition, admitted to trying to manoeuvre a scheme which did not meet the requirements of the brief into the winning position because he recognised that the designer had talent and considered that the problems could be sorted out when commissioned. He was unsuccessful. The jury selected a scheme which, while it lacked the design quality of the other, had succeeded in meeting the brief. The scheme was built and the promoter professed himself well-pleased but the press expressed disappointment. In another case, a team submitting an innovative entry failed to give due weight to another part of the brief which stressed the importance of security. The promoter commented: 'It was an attractive design but on that site the local kids would have had a field day – they would have smashed it up in no time.'

Experience does, however, suggest that the word 'innovative' needs to ring a few warning bells. Some years ago, Northampton County Council was presented with a design for its proposed new headquarters in the form of a multi-storey glass pyramid. The assessors reported that it fulfilled all the requirements of the brief including that for an innovative design. It was never built.

Using the interview procedures

Most competitions introduce interviews and presentations into the process. These may be used either to brief or to assess – or to do both simultaneously. Where they are introduced explicitly as a selection procedure, the number of shortlisted competitors is reduced after the interviews have taken place.

Many promoters use them to supplement the briefing documents. In such situations, they provide an opportunity for competitors to test out ideas and work out priorities. While briefing, the assessors may also be trying to encourage the competitor to develop an aspect of the scheme which they found most interesting and direct them away from a route which they felt was likely to prove less productive. Competitors need to see these interviews as opportunities to collect information which could give them the edge in developing their design proposal rather than as tests of personality.

Where interviews are being used as part of the selection process, the assessors' and/or promoter's interest may only in part be directed towards understanding the design proposal. They are also likely to be assessing the competitors' attitudes and their potential to see the project through to completion. When attitudes are being discussed the term 'flexibility' recurs – the ability to respond and adapt. In many cases the design will have got the competitor to the interview stage. The assessors and/or the promoter will then be probing to find out how good a grasp of the technicalities the architect has, whether the further development of the scheme has been considered in any depth, whether he or she is likely to be able to work alongside the promoter's management team, and how effective the architect would be, if appointed, at taking the project through to completion.

Horses for courses

Competitions are a gamble. Like other forms of gambling the biggest rewards are linked to the greatest risks. A limited or regional competition in a known area of expertise could bring in one acceptable commission. Both the odds and the cost are likely to reasonable. At the other end of the scale, winning an open international competition for a prestige project could change an architect's whole life. The odds, however, may be quite crazy and the cost (in time and effort if not in actual money) horrendous. One glance at the wall of models on display at the Cardiff Bay Opera House Trust competition exhibition (Frontispiece), should be enough to demonstrate the nature of the exercise. No practice can justify a gamble of this nature other than on a very occasional basis.

To bring work into a practice, a balanced package of competitions is required. Many younger architects and less established practices will claim that there are not sufficient numbers of competitions to allow them to plan in this way and that the current situation makes gamblers of them all. This is true. The wide variety of competitions outlined in Chapter 3, are often restricted to already established practices. Where promoters invite entries they tend to limit their considerations to architects who have already built similar projects. With competitions based on an 'invitation to express interest' followed by some form of pre-selection (e.g. South Bank, Durham University, Tate Gallery) experience plays a crucial role. That leaves the relatively few open competitions. As the established practices will also be looking to these to bring in new areas of work, it is difficult for others to make the breakthrough.

Some promoters are beginning to broaden the base on which they operate. More could be encouraged to do so, either through lottery funding procedures or positive initiatives on the part of the design professions.

8 The UK national lottery

The launch of the national lottery in November 1994, heralded what has been described as the largest building programme in sport and the arts for decades. The guidelines for distributing the available funds place an emphasis on quality and competitions are cited as one of the ways of achieving this. Well before the guidelines were published, reports suggested that preference would be given to competition-winning projects with the result that a series of competitions was held, some before any criteria had been established. They included competitions for the South Bank Arts Centre, London; the British Museum Reading Room, London; the Cardiff Bay Opera House; the Baltic Flour Mills Arts Centre, Gateshead; the Tate Gallery's Bankside Museum of Modern Art, London; The National Glass Centre, Sunderland and the Manchester City Art Gallery extension.

The national lottery is co-ordinated by the government through its Office of the National Lottery (OFLOT), which established the legal framework. Bids were invited from potential organisers and in May 1994, the Camelot group was appointed to run the lottery. The money raised is divided in accordance with set criteria amongst the holders of winning tickets; the operators; the government (through a 12% lottery tax); and 'good causes' (28% of the total received). There are five of these: charities, arts, sport, heritage and, for the first five years, projects and events to celebrate the millenium.

The government designated or created a number of organisations to distribute funds in each of these five areas. There are eleven of these 'distributory bodies' covering sports (the Sports Councils of England, Scotland, Wales and Northern Ireland); arts (the Arts Councils of England, Scotland, Wales and Northern Ireland); heritage (the National Heritage Memorial Fund); charities (the Lottery Charities Board) and millenium projects (the Millenium Commission). Each of the distributing bodies publishes its own guidelines and application forms (addresses are given at the end of this chapter).

The potential impact of lottery funding

During the first year of its operation the national lottery is expected to raise in excess of £3 000 million in ticket sales. This figure is based on the average weekly sales during the first three months of operation. As the lottery becomes more established and further games such as scratch cards are introduced the income is expected to increase. Each area of funding, receives an equal share of the 'good causes' money. An annual lottery income of £3 000 million provides a fund of £840 million for distribution which works out at £168 million for each area of funding. A substantial proportion of this money, between 70% and 80%, has been earmarked for capital expenditure. To qualify for lottery funding, many applicants will have to find matching or contributory money from other sources. This requirement could double the amount of money being spent on the designated 'good causes'. It has been heralded as a great building bonanza – a bandwagon on which all architects should jump. Its impact will be significant within the areas it is designated to fund. By way of comparison, the Arts Council's Housing the Arts Fund had a budget of between £1 and £2 million a year until it was abandoned in 1985. The lottery produced this amount of arts capital funding in the first week of its operation. The Sports Council was spending about £10 million a year on building projects before the introduction of lottery funding. Even when considered in the context of the main public capital expenditure heads, the amount is still substantial. Central government capital spending on health projects (1993/94) was £1.1 billion and on education £870 million (with local authority expenditure accounting for a further £931 million). The Department of National Heritage which covers many of the areas to which lottery funding is to be allocated, had a capital budget of £300 million in 1994/95 (although a sizeable chunk of this was for the British Library building).

The capital funds to be provided by the lottery income will not, however, be limited to expenditure on new buildings and improved accommodation. Just how much money will be spent in this way requires careful analysis. The only body not instructed to concentrate on capital funding is the Lottery Charities Board. All the others are to direct their funding to this end. But included within the terms of reference are equipment, land acquisition and preparation (e.g. sites of particular interest in the case of the National Heritage Memorial Fund and tracks, pitches, bridleways and fishing rights with the Sports Councils), heritage works and objects of value; start-up funding and the occasional endowment.

Distribution criteria

The basis on which the lottery operates was established by the National Lottery Act 1993. This created the distributory bodies and set out their terms of reference but did not attempt to designate selection criteria.

Prompted by an open letter from a number of design and environmental organisations, the Secretary of State for National Heritage (then Peter Brooke) wrote to the distributory bodies outlining the criteria he expected them to take into account when selecting recipients for lottery funding. He cited a number of considerations including:

- the need for all buildings to be well-designed, well constructed, of high quality and fit for purpose;
- the need to avoid short-term savings which would obscure the positive benefits of good design and fitness for purpose;
- the need to ensure that new buildings and refurbishments are environmentally friendly, energy efficient and that their style complements the character of the locality and the nature of the assets and facilities they house.

A working party was set up to look at how this advice could best be implemented. It was convened by the Architecture Unit of the Arts Council and included representatives from other distributing bodies (National Heritage Memorial Fund, The Sports Council and the Scottish Arts Council) as well as from English Heritage, the Royal Fine Art Commission and the RIBA. The result of these discussions was a report 'National Lottery architecture and construction advice for capital projects', published in October 1994. The report recommended that distributors adopt common policies to ensure high standards of design, construction quality and performance. One such policy was that the distributors 'insist on architectural competitions for appropriate capital projects where the lottery contributes at least £1 million of capital funds'.

The report is considered to be an advisory document and it is left to the individual distributory bodies to decide how best to implement its recommendations. The general principles are endorsed by all the bodies responsible for distributing capital funds, including the Millenium Commission which was still in the process of being set up when the working group met.

The emphasis on design quality

All the distributory bodies have set quality of design and construction as a criteria for selection.

The Millenium Commission, for example, includes the statement: 'In making its choice between different proposals for millenium projects, the Commission will seek projects which are of high architectural and design quality.' The Sports Council documents advise, 'A key objective for Lottery Sports Fund projects is that they should be of high quality, well designed and constructed, and able to stand up to many years of hard enjoyable use.' The Scottish Arts Council document heads one paragraph, 'High standards of design and architecture are to be applied' and goes on to explain that, 'the pursuit of excellence in design and architecture is a specific goal of the Scottish Arts Council'.

All the bodies distributing funds for building projects are prepared to consider applications for grants towards the cost of feasibility studies and competitions directed towards achieving high levels of design quality (1995 applications). The only exception is the National Heritage Memorial Fund which anticipates relatively little expenditure on new buildings during the first years of operation.

The distributory bodies consider that they have a role as patrons. This view is held most strongly by the arts organisations, who consider the art of architecture to fall within their area of responsibility. This has led them to take the lead in working out methods of securing quality of design in lottery projects.

The distributory bodies have another equally if not more important reason for placing so strong an emphasis on design quality. They take the view that design quality, and the quality of the construction and materials used, extend the useful life of a building and reduce the ongoing maintenance requirements.

The introductory sections to the 1994 report make the case for a joint architectural policy, concluding with the following statement:

> If the lifetime cost of a building is 100%, its capital cost is only 10%. Yet its design cost is a mere 1%, even though the quality of this initial design thinking determines a building's usefulness and its overall artistic merit. Making time for design can save money later. Paying properly for design is a wise investment. Good architecture does not cost more than bad, measured at the lifetime level. In fact, it should cost less and will certainly deliver more value.

The report identifies architectural competitions as one of the key means of securing the design quality sought.

The public interest

There is one criteria which has to be met before any other considerations are brought into play. It relates to the concept of 'public good' and stresses relevance, accessibility, and proven need. It involves public consultation and public participation. The Sports Council guidelines state:

> We will favour projects that cater for the widest possible cross-section of the community. The stated purpose of the Lottery is to make important and long-lasting differences to the quality of life, and to promote the public good. So it

follows that the more people from all walks of life that your proposed project would reach, the more chance it has of success. . . . Clearly, the more support there is for your project, the more chance there is that we can support it too, with Lottery funding.

The Millenium Commission lists two key criteria which applications must meet before any other considerations are brought into play. These are that the project must:

- enjoy public support;
- make a substantial contribution to the life of the community it is designed to serve.

The need to ensure that the money serves the public good is the main principle in the distribution of lottery funds.

The role of competitions

The distributing bodies are conscious of the fact that their funding represents public patronage for building projects at a very significant level. There are few precedents for them to follow. In the early years of lottery funding, all procedures will be seen as 'experimental', testing different approaches and subject to review and adaptation as experience is accumulated.

The initial 'competitions push' is already being modified to a certain extent and even where it is a stated requirement some flexibility is being observed. At the same time, the case for architectural competitions is a very strong one. Anything which looks like backtracking on the original intent is probably attributable more to the initial problems of implementating a competition-based system than to doubts as to its relevance.

One of the strongest arguments in favour of competitions for the distributions of lottery funding is that of public interest. This relates to the need to ensure that public money is distributed fairly, that the facilities provided are what the public wants and that buildings erected within the public realm are welcome additions to the environment.

Although these conditions can be met in a variety of ways, the competition system offers unique opportunities for participation and consultation as well as a set of procedures specifically designed to be demonstrably fair and open.

Promoting the use of architectural competitions can also be seen to fulfil the objective of patronage. When well and sensitively run, competitions can have two key roles. One is to secure quality and the other is to identify and encourage new talent. Whereas there are several procedures which can be used to select a good architect from amongst known names, the only tried and tested way of directing work to younger and less established architects is through the competition system.

The distributing bodies are also aware of the EC directives and their guidelines draw the attention of applicants to the requirements. For example, the Millenium Commission guidance notes state:

> Applicants for Millenium Commission funds must have regard to European Community procurement legislation . . . You will be required to ensure that you are fully aware of the implications of the legislation as it applies to your project when you submit a full application to the Commission.

This is an important area which may have an increasing influence in the future. It already draws a number of lottery projects into some form of competitive selection procedure, even where there is no competition requirement specified by the distributing organisation (see Chapter 9).

Several of the distributory bodies are looking at the competition system and at other ways of selecting architects which would meet their criteria with a view to drawing up guidelines for lottery applicants. The first sets of guidelines should be available by the end of 1995.

Existing requirements

In the first year of operation, a study of the application packs shows that only one of the distributing bodies has given full force to the working party's recommendation in respect of competitions – the Arts Council of England. In its document 'Detailed Guidance to applicants' it states:

> For building projects which need more than £100 000 of lottery funding we will give priority to projects which are based on a successful feasibility study and a suitable design competition. If your project needs more than £1 million of lottery funding, you must carry out both a feasibility study and a design competition or you must provide a full explanation of why these steps are not appropriate for your project.
>
> You can apply for lottery funds towards the costs of the early development stages of a project, including feasibility studies, briefing and design competitions. Receiving a grant for these purposes will not reduce your chance of receiving a second grant, at a later date, towards the cost of completing the project.

Where the architect was appointed prior to the issue of the application pack in November 1994, these requirements do not apply. The Arts Council has also indicated that it will consider applications which do not follow this requirement provided the applicants can give a good reason for not doing so.

In its first set of documentation, the Arts Council does not seek either to define the term 'design competition' or to outline basic requirements. Its application pack includes a number of advisory documents, one of which, 'Arts Buildings: Suggestions for successful management of capital projects', includes a section on competitions. It states:

> As ways of commissioning buildings increase, a wide choice of competitive procedures for selecting architects is emerging. Different approaches are appropriate in different situations.

It stresses the need for competitions to be conducted to high standards of integrity and professionalism and focusses on the importance of public consultation. It would appear that many of the competition formats outlined in Chapter 3 could fulfil the Arts Council's requirements for a design competition. Fee bidding would be excluded as it contains no design element. A careful reading of both the document within the application pack and the earlier report suggests that either the traditional architectural competition or one of the modified formats offered by the professional institutes would be favoured as would a carefully organised selection procedure. The competitive interview (see page 27) may also become accepted if guidelines can be agreed.

The Scottish Arts Council has taken a more relaxed view. For projects in receipt of funding of over £1 million, competitions are recommended but not mandatory. For smaller projects, the process by which an architect is selected is left to the discretion of the client body. Where a competition is held, the RIAS will consider applications towards the cost, provided that it follows the RIAS guidelines. Before producing its lottery documentation, the Scottish Arts Council held a series of seminars with architects throughout the country. It found that there was considerable opposition to the 'unofficial' competition system being developed in England (i.e. selection procedure formats organised without RIBA endorsement) and fears that if these unregulated procedures were to be accepted in Scotland they could discredit the well-established RIAS system.

A similar approach is be taken by both the Welsh Arts Council and the Arts Council of Northern Ireland who are discussing the competition issue with their respective architectural institutes. The Welsh Arts Council has 'neither endorsed nor not endorsed' this aspect of the guidance document (February 1995). It is working on its own guidelines for competitions and expects to have them available by the second year of the lottery operation. The Arts Council of Northern Ireland is 'expecting' organisations applying for funds in excess of £1 million to 'consider' promoting a competition. The Royal Society of Ulster Architects, like the RIAS, is wary of the 'designer selection method' style of competition and may well advise against its use.

The Millenium Commission which, unlike the Sports and Arts bodies, was not grafted on to an existing organisation is less advanced in its policy development. While it endorses the requirements for public acceptability and for quality it is still studying how these might best be achieved.

Potential problems

One of the strengths of the lottery system – that of providing capital funding for a wide range of independent organisations – is also a potential source of problems. As one commentator observed, 'Procurement is in the hands of people who don't know anything about it – there is a real risk that lottery money will not be well spent if people do not know how to purchase from the construction industry.' Although all the distributing bodies have guidance notes on project development in their application packs, it is generally recognised that more advisory and support services need to be developed.

There are fears amongst the architectural profession that the competition requirement may be misinterpreted and lead to an increased demand for competitive work against poorly thought out or changing briefs.

For architects the combination of competition and lottery could involve a double gamble. Firstly they are required to compete for a commission and then to compete for funding before any fees can be secured. (The funding for housing association work follows a similar pattern and has proved a source of complaint and conflict for more than a decade.)

In some cases, architects have established working relationships with local arts, sports or heritage organisations and both parties have invested time and effort in working out what is required. When the client does not have design and/or building expertise within its own organisation or does not have the money to appoint consultants when a building project is first being considered, this type of relationship often provides the best route forward. Introducing a competition into such a situation is unlikely to prove productive unless the client is seeking a way out of the existing relationship.

Recent experience has shown a marked preference for promoters to select only from amongst the known and established. While this is understandable in the early stages of lottery funding, it could become a source of contention if the pattern continues too far into the future.

Options and opportunities

There is a strong case for arguing that the interests of all those concerned are best served by combining a selective and regulated use of the competition system with a standard procedure which does not require design work to be undertaken before the commission is offered.

Selective use of the competition system means that promoters who find its terms unacceptable or its formats too restrictive are free to choose other methods. This is likely to prove preferable in the long term to forcing the system on unwilling promoters (who will not build if they do not like the result) or attempting to adapt it to meet requirements which lie outside its scope.

Regulated use of the system means that the so called 'rogue' competitions are discouraged, that the amount of wasted effort is kept to the minimum, that work is distributed more widely, that the results of the system are publicised and that the experience gained is made available to future promoters.

The distributory bodies have already established that they regard money and time spent in developing the design as crucial to the quality of the end product – the building. They have also determined that the money is to go to a wide range of projects; of different type, scale and with a wide geographical spread. Each is to be treated as a 'one-off'; planned, developed and designed to respond to the needs of the local community and of the area in which it is to be built. These attitudes provide the climate in which architectural competitions can flourish.

By offering to fund competitions, the distributory bodies are also in a position to discriminate in favour of those which serve a particular set of requirements. Design quality is one. Public participation is already established as another. In establishing these criteria, two of the key objectives of the architectural competition system have already been met. A third objective, and one which is considered by many to be equally important, is that of opening the selection process to new design solutions, new ideas and new talent. This does not mean that all competitions would have to be reserved for the inexperienced and unproven. The architectural competition system is designed to test the new against the already established and accepted. It is a case of widening opportunities within a context which is relevant to each particular project. Recent competition experience shows that this is unlikely to happen automatically. Ways will need to be found of introducing promoters to a wider range of potential designers, if the third objective of the architectural competition system is to be achieved.

Documentation and distributing bodies

Documentation

- National Lottery Act 1993. Chapter 39 published by HMS0 (1993).
- National Lottery architecture and construction advice published by The Arts Council of England (1994).
- Application and information packs published by the individual distributory bodies 1994/95.

Distributory bodies

The Sports Council, 16 Upper Woburn Place, London WC1H 0QP. For sports projects in England. Tel: 0345 649 649.

The Scottish Sports Council, Caledonia House, South Gyle, Edinburgh EH12 9DQ. For sports projects in Scotland. Tel: 0131 226 6051.

The Sports Council for Wales, Welsh Institute of Sport, Sophia Gardens, Cardiff CF1 9SW. For sports projects in Wales. Tel: 01222 397 571.

The Sports Council for Northern Ireland, House of Sport, Upper Malone Road, Belfast BT9 5LA. For sports projects in Northern Ireland. Tel: 01232 382 222.

The Millenium Commission, 2 Little Smith Street, London SW1P 3DH. For projects to mark the year 2000 and the beginning of the third millenium throughout the UK. Tel: 0171 340 2001.

The National Heritage Memorial Fund, 10 St James's Street, London SW1A 1EF. For built heritage, conservation and preservation projects, museums and galleries and national heritage throughout the UK. Tel: 0171 649 1345.

The National Lottery Charities Board, 7th floor, St Vincent House, 30 Orange Street, London WC2H 7HH. For grants to charities, voluntary organisations and organisations with a philanthropic aim throughout the UK. Tel: 0171 839 5371.

The Arts Council of England, 14 Great Peter Street, London SW1P 3NQ. For arts projects in England. Tel: 0171 312 0123.

The Scottish Arts Council, 12 Manor Place, Edinburgh EH3 7DD. For arts projects in Scotland. Tel: 0131 226 6051.

The Arts Council of Wales, Holst House, Museum Place, Cardiff CF1 3NX. For arts projects in Wales. Tel: 01222 394 711.

The Arts Council of Northern Ireland, 185 Stranmillis Road, Belfast BT9 5DU. For arts projects in Northern Ireland. Tel: 01232 677 000.

9 The European open market

As Europe becomes more integrated, the practices of one area begin to impinge on what happens elsewhere. This is both a formal and informal process. The formal structures of the European Union are working towards a unified set of standards and procedures. The reciprocal recognition of qualifications and the opening of markets facilitates the movement of the workforce and with this the dissemination of working practices.

The 'competition countries' taken en bloc are increasingly influential within the European Union. This influence is apparent in the rules for 'design contests' in the EC directive governing the procurement of services.

The procurement legislation

European legislation now covers the way goods, works and services are commissioned throughout the European Union. The rules apply both to public bodies and to some individual projects where public money is involved (see below). The rules come into effect once stated cost 'thresholds' are passed. These currently (1995) stand at 5 million ECU (approximately £3.5 million) for public works contracts (e.g. buildings) and 200 000 ECU (approximately £150 000) for public services contracts. Design and consultancy work is regarded as a service.

The information which follows is a guide to the context in which most publicly funded organisations are now required to operate. European legislation is complicated and much of it is open to interpretation. Organisations which fall within the jurisdiction of this legislation (perhaps through a single project) and are unfamilar with EC requirements may need to take legal advice.

Legislation passed by the European Parliament is given force in the UK under the terms of the 1972 European Communities Act. It comes in the form of 'directives'. The governments of the member states are required to draw up rules for the implementation of the directives in their individual countries. The rules drawn up by the member states are referred to as 'secondary legislation' and become part of the law of each individual state. In the UK, this legislation takes the form of statutory instruments (SIs).

Over the last few years, legislation has been introduced to harmonise procedures for the award of contracts and to assist in the free movement of goods and services within the European Union. Collectively these are referred to as 'the EC procurement rules'. They cover both building contracts and design services and are legally binding. Public bodies and organisations substantially financed by public funds are bound by these rules, as are organisations providing certain public utilities. The rules may also apply to single projects where more than 50% of the costs are met from public funds. Though funding policies are still being developed, it seems likely that some projects seeking national lottery money will fall into this category.

One set of rules spells out the procedures which have to be followed when design services are being sought. All these procedures include an element of competition. Design contests are identified as one of the accepted selection methods and the documents set out rules for their organisation. Any competitions which adhere to the guidelines drawn up by the IUA or ACE (Architects Council of Europe in this context) will fulfil EC requirements. The professional institutes listed on page 42 also offer suitable formats. Those seeking to adapt these guidelines or draw up their own competition conditions are recommended to take legal advice to ensure that they are operating within the appropriate EC directive.

The regulations governing public services came into force on 13 January 1994 which means that the construction industry is still coming to terms with the implications and working out how the rules relate to specific situations. Interpretations of the regulations which have been made have not, as yet, been tested by law. No 'aggrieved supplier' has taken a case to court. Should this happen in the future and should the court conclude that there had been a failure of duty, it could suspend the contract (if there was still time) or award damages (possibly to cover loss of profit or to reimburse expenses). More importantly, the whole contract could be delayed while the case was sorted out.

Documentation

The procurement regulations apply when public authorities (called 'contracting authorities') acquire goods, works and services from 'service providers'. There are three sets of regulations, one for each of the following areas:

- Supplies (purchase or hire of goods);
- Works (civil engineering and building services);
- Services (this is the one which covers the commissioning of architects and all design and building consultants).

A fourth set of regulations covers all three areas and applies only to companies dealing in the provision of utlities (energy, water, transport and telecommunications).

The document covering design services is 'The Public Services Contracts Regulations 1993 (SI 1993/3228)'. It can be obtained from HMSO. Where explanatory information is quoted in this chapter it is taken from this document unless otherwise indicated.

Definitions of 'public bodies'

The contracting authorities are defined in the Regulations. Many are defined by what they are (e.g. government, local authority) but a test of source of funds also draws in others, including most of the quangos. Universities, colleges and some museums are regarded as 'contracting authorities' whereas most charities and charitable trusts are not (for instance the National Trust is not considered to be a contracting authority.) Nationalised industries are excluded (under provisions relating to industrial and commercial organisations) though certain privatised industries are brought in under the terms of the 'Utilities SI'. The government has produced a booklet 'Public Bodies' (drawn up by the Cabinet Office) which lists public bodies under the headings of the appropriate funding departments. Where an organisation is unsure of its position, it should seek the advice of the public body from which it receives its main funding.

Definitions of 'publicly funded' projects

There are clauses in the regulations related to 'subsidised works contracts' which apply where a contracting authority undertakes to contribute 'more than half of the consideration to be or expected to be paid under a contract'. This applies to 'a contract which would be a public works contract if the subsidised body were a contracting authority' and relates to 'the carrying out of building works for hospitals, facilities intended for sports, recreation and leisure, school and university building or buildings for administrative purposes'.

Lottery grants

All the eleven distributory bodies for the national lottery funds are 'contracting authorities'. Any organisation receiving a grant from one of these bodies which accounts for more than 50% of the anticipated cost of the contract, is likely to be regarded as a 'contracting authority' for the project to which the grant relates. If the project crosses one of the EC cost 'thresholds', the organisation will be bound to follow the regulations for the procurement of services. The figure of 50% relates to the percentage contribution made towards the cost of the specific project and not to the amount of annual revenue subsidy an organisation might receive. Whether the 50% figure refers to a single grant or an accumulated fund (e.g. lottery plus central government plus local authority contributions) appears not, as yet, to be fully determined but it is probably advisable to assume that it does.

Design fee threshold

For the purposes of the EC directive, the term services includes: 'Architectural services: engineering services and integrated engineering services, urban planning and landscape architectural services; related scientific and technical consulting services; technical testing and analysis services.' The regulations come into effect when a commission is offered in excess of the threshold figure of 200 000 ECU. Depending on how the appointments are made, this figure could relate to each individual fee or could be regarded as applying to the fee for the team as a unit. There are rules covering 'aggregation' to prevent clients from splitting up contracts into a series of small units. Clarification of this issue could be a legal matter.

Procedures to be followed

The procedures fall into three basic categories: open, restricted or negotiated. There is also a 'design contest' option. In all these procedures the contracting authority is required to place a notice in the *Official Journal of the European Communities* setting out the basis on which the contract is offered and the criteria which have to be met.

> **Open:** The open procedure relates to 'fee bid' system. How this system operates is explained on page 20. The *EC Journal* announcement invites tenders for the work. The regulations allow the contracting authority to exclude from consideration any tenders which fail a particular set of tests. These tests relate to 'economic and financial standing' and to 'ability and technical capacity' and have to be applied on a non-discriminatory basis. (The discrimination the EC seeks to preclude is one based on state or nationality.) Once these basic exclusion tests have

been applied, the contract is then offered to the 'services provider' submitting the lowest tender.

Restricted: The restricted procedures still require an announcement to be placed in the *EC Journal* but allow the contracting authority to limit the number of participants submitting a tender. Where a range is stated it has to be between 5 and 20. The participants can be selected from the initial trawl of interest on any basis provided it is 'non-discriminatory'. Tests can be applied as above to exclude unsuitable applicants before any selection process takes place. The contract can be awarded either on a lowest cost basis (as in the open procedure) or on the basis of 'the most economically advantageous'. The criteria which can be used to determine which is the most economically advantageous include 'quality, aesthetic and functional characteristics and technical merit'.

Negotiated: The negotiated procedures relate to situations where the number of potential suppliers is limited (i.e. in very specialised areas of consultancy or for very large or complicated design projects). The contracting authority is required to negotiate with a minimum of three suppliers to ensure competition. Regulations covering exclusion apply as above.

Design contests

The regulations apply to a design contest when it leads either to the award of a contract in excess of 200 000 ECU or where the value of prizes and payments is in excess of this figure.

Promoters are required to:

- place an announcement in the *EC Journal*.
- make available the rules to anyone expressing an interest.
- appoint a jury which is independent of participants in the contest. Where a particular professional qualification is required from contestants, at least one third of the jury members must have a comparable qualification.
- submit the contestants' proposals to the jury 'without any indication as to the authorship of each proposal'.
- ensure that the jury makes its decisions independently and solely on the basis of the criteria set out in the *EC Journal* notice.

The promoter is permitted to restrict the number of persons invited to participate, provided that the selection is made on the basis of 'clear and non discriminatory criteria'.

There are no situations in which it is obligatory to hold a design contest but where one is held, the above rules apply.

A professionally based consultative group has been set up to co-ordinate response to the EC legislation – the Architects Council of Europe (ACE). It has produced rules for the conduct of competitions for architects in the EC countries but these are not, as yet, widely available. They are currently regarded as providing guidelines for the professional organisations and competition committees in the individual member countries.

The system in use

One of the key problems with the EC procedures is the cost and work involved in administering the Europe-wide invitation. The 'open' system does not commend itself to many organisations commissioning design services as it commits the contracting agency to select on the basis of the lowest fee bid. Most contracting agencies use the restricted procedures as these permit a range of criteria to be taken into consideration. Both these procedures, and the procedures for any type of design contest, have to be announced in the *EC Journal* so that architects throughout Europe can express interest. Response rates can be high. A contracting agency may be required to send out several hundred packs of information even when it intends to select only six or ten service providers to tender. Similarly, a limited competition has to be preceded by a trawl of interest. There is also a time factor to be taken into account. Contracting authorities are required to allow a period of 37 days between despatch of the notification to the *EC Journal* and the selection of suppliers. (Note: the relevant date is the date of despatch, by post or fax, not the date on which the announcement appears in the journal.) Thereafter, the contracting agency is required to allow a further 40 days for submissions to be prepared. These are minimum times. An 'accelerated procedure' is available but only in special circumstances. It is also possible to reduce the 40 day period by issuing an 'indicative notice'.

Organisations are beginning to define their selection criteria more carefully. Although the *EC Journal* is required to delete any restrictions which it considers to conflict with the directives, criteria such as 'prepared to establish an operating base in the area' and 'comprising multi-disciplinary teams with experience of similar scale projects' have been passed. The guidance is that they should be 'performance specific' rather than 'proscriptive'. The main requirement is that any restrictions which are imposed are clearly stated and are non-discriminatory, in EC terms. Where a small number of service providers is being selected, discrimination on the grounds of state and nationality can be difficult to prove. An organisation which may have come close to facing this charge (though for reasons quite opposite to those envisaged by the EC legislation) was the Tate Gallery when it excluded all UK architects except one, when selecting from a trawl with a predominant UK base. The key rule seems to be that the selection must be made against acceptable and stated criteria and the contracting agency must be able to defend the basis on which it is made.

Several organisations have promoted 'competitions' since these rules came into force which have not followed the format outlined in the 'design contest' rules. These appear to have been organised by interpreting procedures set out in the procurement documents which permit selection to be made on the basis of 'the most economically advantageous'. As these allow a number of design-related criteria to be taken into account, it can be argued that the contracting agency needs to look at design approaches in order to make the assessment. In some cases the promoter has avoided the term 'competition' and made reference to a 'selection procedure'. This may come to be regarded as the accepted terminology.

Architects tend to view the opportunities offered in the *EC Journal* with some suspicion. They suspect that in situations other than an open design contest the selection has already been made. Random discussions with UK promoters reinforces this view. One commented, 'the EC requirement did not make the slightest difference – except for the delay and extra work involved'. When asked whether the preferred architects had been specifically invited to express interest, another promoter replied, 'No, but we might mention the EC advertisement to them or send them a photocopy of the page it was on.' Although these attitudes conflict with the spirit of EC legislation and if made explicit, could lead to action be taken to question the legality of the resulting service commission, it would seem likely that contracting authorities throughout Europe are applying similar methods in order to ensure that the people they want are included in any list of service providers.

The Department of Trade and Industry carried out a study (1994) which showed that there was very little penetration of the UK market for either goods or services with 96% of all contracts within the UK going to UK-based firms. This experience is mirrored in the procurement of architectural and design services. Even with open entry design competitions, the response from non-UK architects has not been great though there are now more cross national links between practices. The competition promoted by the University of Durham, for example, attracted 149 responses. Relatively few (eleven) were from non UK architects and most of these were intending to work in association with UK-based practices. This situation may change as both contracting authorities and service providers gain more experience in the open market.

10 The competition system in Europe

The competition system is well established in Europe and within the European Union countries but its use is not evenly spread. For many years, competitions tended to be associated with the Scandinavian and German speaking countries. In the 1970s, between 200 and 400 competitions were held each year in Germany and between 70 and 100 in Switzerland. Each of the Scandinavian countries held about 10 a year and France and the UK each managed five or so. The system was virtually ignored in both southern and eastern European countries, except for the occasional grand gesture of an international competition.

Procedures and practice

In overall terms, the situation has changed very little except for one country, France. During the 1970s, the competition system began to be used to select architects and designers for the 'grands projets' (a series of one-off public buildings) and was then developed for hundreds of 'petits projets' for smaller public and publicly financed buildings such as schools, hospitals and housing units throughout France. Although the French example is frequently cited as one to be followed, no detailed studies of how the change was achieved or what its relevance might be to the UK have been undertaken. The Department of National Heritage, when headed by Peter Brooke, began to look at the concept of government-led 'grands projets' but any reports which were produced were kept for internal consideration only. The official view could be regarded as that given by Peter Brooke when he opened the exhibition 'Architectures Capitales à Paris' (held at the RIBA in July 1994). He said:

French practice has a heavy emphasis on design competitions as a way of identifying fresh talent. We in Britian have had a less happy experience of competitions, which have not always yielded sensible and worthwhile results. There is, as a result, some scepticism about the process. But there is a variety of ways in which competitions can be mounted. We need to persevere, particularly on major public buildings where it is right to consider a wide range of design options.

All the competition systems follow a similar pattern (that of the traditional architectural competition outlined on page 43) and use the same basic set of procedures. The anonymity requirement is standard and most systems require professional members to be in the majority on the jury, though some of them may be appointed by the promoter. Most countries leave the regulation of competitions to the relevant professional institutes, occasionally with the rules endorsed by an appropriate government department. In most cases a competitions committee is established to check conditions against the standard regulations, to nominate one or two jury members and to act as a court of appeal in cases of dispute. The Finnish system requires promoters to sign a formal agreement undertaking to follow the regulations in all respects. The Dutch system is regulated by a pan-institute committee with its membership drawn from eight different arts, architecture and design organisations. What differences there are relate to detail and emphasis rather than to substance. Though there is some scope for exchange of ideas, these differences are not sufficient to account for wide variations in the use of the architectural competition system.

Where competitions are used most extensively (e.g. Austria, Finland and Germany) it is because they have become part of the culture of these countries. (The only exception to this generalisation is France, where legislation was used to create a competition culture.) Factors such as government and local government responsibilities, sources of funding, traditions of patronage all play a part. Differences in the practice of architecture and the structure of the design professions also have an important role, although whether these differences come under the heading of 'cause' or of 'effect' is open to discussion. In many European countries the design stages of a building project tend to be seen as one distinct process. The design studios take the clients' brief and develop the design proposal and then work as consultants to in-house teams who are responsible for getting the design built. In France, for instance, drawing up the brief has become a specialised area of work. In Germany, public authority teams oversee the tender and building stages. In the UK the role of the architect has traditionally been that of 'team leader' taking the building project right through from conception to completion. Some argue that this way of working precludes a more extensive use of the competition system in this country. Others claim that the climate in which architects operate is the discriminatory factor, not the way they practice. The different perception of the architect's role may, however, explain why the UK has developed a far more flexible competition system than those of other European countries.

The introduction of the EC procurement rules is leading many European countries to assess their competition systems. The Bund Deutscher Architekten (the German Institute of Architects) is looking at how the EC requirements can be accommodated within its own strong regional system. In the past, nearly all competitions have been organised by the Länder (the German regions) with many of them restricted to architects practising within their areas. The same problem will face Austria when it is required to introduce the procurement rules into its own legislation in 1996 and the Finns are concerned that they will be asked to implement procedures which they have previously considered and rejected as inappropriate.

In the longer term, the advent of the open market is likely to lead both to more competitions and to them being more evenly spread throughout the European Union. The current discrepancies of opportunity have been noted and are a matter of concern in those countries which offer the most open competition systems. For example, a spokesperson for the Bund Deutscher Architekten writes:

> ... architects from Europe as well as other countries all over the world participate in large numbers in competitions organised in the Federal Republic of Germany. We do support this open-mindedness as a basis for an intellectual competition aiming at high quality and the best architectural solutions. Vice-versa, we would also appreciate it if German architects were admitted and welcome to take part in competitions organised by other countries.

Patterns of use

Although EC legislation is working to even out differences of practice throughout Europe, there are factors in each country which affect how competitions are organised. Competition use and practice tends to divide the European countries into a number of groups reflecting historic, legislative or language links.

France

The competition system in France is administered jointly by the Ordre des Architects (the professional institute) and the Mission interministerielle pour la qualité des constructions publiques (MIQCP, an interdepartmental agency within the government). The law requires specified competition procedures to be used for a wide range of public engineering and architectural commissions (introduced in 1986 and amended in 1993). The commissioning figure above when such procedures become compulsory is set at 900 000 F. Legislation defines the range of public buildings covered (these include government and local authority funded buildings in health, education and housing); the duties and responsibilities of the public officials charged with overseeing the projects; the procedures to be followed; and the composition and duties of the jury. The relevant regulations come under the heading of 'La Maitrise d'ouvrage publique' (rules governing public works), referred to as the MOP rules.

In 1994, the Ordre des Architects reported approximately 2000 competitions were being organised on average each year and estimated that 90% of them resulted in the project being built. The regional system is not used in France.

Germany, Austria and Switzerland

Between 400 and 600 competitions are organised in Germany every year. In the past most of these were promoted within one of the Länder. The number of competitions held in the different regions varies widely. Though this relates in part to population and the number of buildings being commissioned, it also reflects the prevailing traditions and attitudes. (The competition rules are more or less standard throughout Germany.) In 1992, for example, 138 competitions were held in Nordrhein-Westfalen and 122 in Baden-Wurttenberg compared with 29 in Hessen and 4 in Bremen. Since the EC service directive was issued, a larger proportion of these have been national and Eurowide. German architects still work to a mandatory fee scale and membership of one of the Chambers of Architects (architectural institutes based on the Länder) is obligatory.

In Austria, the competition system is run by the Federal Chamber of Architects and Engineers. There is no legal requirement for architects to be selected by this means but the system is widely used. There are about 70 competitions a year most of which are regional (38%) or invited (54%). Regional competitions can be organised on the basis of a town or community.

A similar system operates in Switzerland where there are some 130 competitions held each year. About half of these are regional competitions (based on the cantons) and half by invitation – with only three or four open to the whole country. Most competitions are run in accordance with regulations drawn up by the SIA (Swiss Union of Engineers and Architects).

Scandinavia

The Scandinavian countries are currently suffering a severe depression in construction (figures indicate that it is worse than that which hit the UK in the early 1990s) and this is affecting the number of competitions held. In Finland, for instance, where the competition system is widely considered to be the cornerstone of its architectural development, the number is down to single figures. (This contrasts with the 40 competitions which were held in 1988.) When operating effectively, the system is used not only for large public buildings but for a whole range of smaller schemes, both public and private (73% central and local government, 17% private and 10% church authorities). The current rules are approved by both the Finnish Association of Architects and, since 1986, jointly by the Finnish Association of Building Proprietors.

The Netherlands

A country which is sometimes cited as offering well-run competitions is the Netherlands, though both the competition system and the climate in which it operates appear to be very similar to those in the UK. The Bond van Nederlandse Architekten (BNA, the architectural institute) writes, 'To our regret our government has neither drawn up any regulations, nor created a competent authority governing architectural competitions.' The regulations are administered by a consortium of design interests – the Permanent Competitions Committee (PPC). Members of the institutes are debarred from entering or acting as assessors on competitions which have not been approved by the PPC. As in the UK, there are no sanctions to enforce this rule.

One difference is that the jury, appointed by the promoter, must contain a majority of design professionals. Until 1992, the promoter had to accept the jury's winner. After studying competition documents from a number of countries, the BNA decided to introduce the UK promoter choice procedures. This is now part of its system.

About 10 competitions a year are organised in accordance with the regulations. As in the UK, many clients use a selection procedure in which two or more architects are invited to submit designs. Members are supposed to inform the BNA when asked to work in this way so that rules regarding proper remuneration can be applied. This system appears to work about as effectively as it did in the UK.

One of the reasons the Dutch system is admired could be accounted for by the outstanding successes gained by young UK architects entering the Europan competition, which enabled some to set up in practice in the country. In fact, the organisers were quite disturbed by this phenomenon especially as various other participating countries had managed to select only compatriots. The Chairman of Europan Nederland writes, 'That the jury's choices ultimately and unexpectedly led to a predominance of Anglo-Saxon winners and honourable mentions (7 out of 10) is remarkable. Is the grass greener over here? Is the education there better geared to the questions raised? Is there a like-mindedness? Questions which demand further study...'

Eastern Europe

Although activity has been limited in the past, a number of eastern European counties are exploring the role of competitions and introducing regulations.

In Hungary, there are now about 40 to 50 competitions a year. Many of these are ideas competitions which are followed by other selection procedures. No formal structure exists although the Chamber of Architects expects legislation governing public spending (scheduled to be introduced in 1995) to include regulation of the competition system.

The Czech Chamber of Architects, set up in 1992, has already drawn up regulations for competitions. These are binding on its members but not on competition promoters and have no legal status at present.

In Romania, the Ministry of Public Works and Town and Regional Planning has introduced legislation requiring competitions to be held to select architects for public buildings. Regulations have been drawn up, in collaboration with the Union of Architects in Romania, based on the IUA (International Union of Architects) documents and specifications. Competitions for public buildings are organised by the Ministry or by local authorities. Those for private buildings are administered by the Union. About twenty competitions have been held but no figures are available as to the number of projects which have been built.

The Europan competition

The Europan competition is one of the few international competition initiatives to have been developed in recent years. It is an open competition for young architects which draws in countries from the whole of Europe. Organised on a biennial basis, 1995 marks the launch of the fourth competition – Europan 4.

The background is set out in a publication featuring the results of Europan 3:

> In 1988, a network of professionals created a European architecture competition federation. The concept was simple; to organise, in each participating country, an ideas competition followed by constructions. Europan had a rapid success with young architects, because of its very principle: first, to give these young architects a shop window for their ideas; and second, to transform these ideas into buildings constructed through a process in which the competition project is confronted with reality.

Europan is open to all European (not just EU) architects under 40 years old, who may choose a site from a range of about 50 possibilities put forward by European towns. A common theme is selected and all competitors work to common rules. By the time the results of Europan 3 were known (end 1994), some 80 projects from the previous two competitions were in the construction phase with 50 nearing completion.

There is considerable interest in this competition amongst young UK architects as it offers one of the few opportunities for open competition. The UK only has associate membership of Europan and did not provide a site for any of the first three competitions. It is being pressured by other organising countries to take a more active role and, working through the RIBA, plans to identify at least one site for the Europan 4 competition. Full membership confers voting rights but also requires a substantially increased contribution and a commitment to identify a minimum of four competition sites.

The competition is significant in that it offers younger architects real opportunities, focusses attention on issues relating to the urban environ-ment and spreads competition expertise throughout the countries of Europe. It could serve as a model for similar intitiatives to be organised at a national level within the UK.

11 Case studies

The remainder of this book is dedicated to nine case studies. The studies have been selected to illustrate different competition procedures covering a range of projects in terms of scope, size and function. These criteria were regarded as more important than geographical spread, though an attempt was made to take examples from different parts of the country.

The promoting bodies include local authorities, a housing association, a university, a charitable trust, arts organisations, an amenity society and a health authority. All are UK based, though several of the competitions are European or international in their scope.

The case studies should not be seen as formats to be followed as their success was due to a large extent to the care each organisation took to tailor the system to suit its own individual requirements. Nor should they be seen as 'exemplary' in the sense that they escaped all problems and attracted no criticism. One led to the resignation of the Prince of Wales as President of its Patrons. One has been criticised for choosing an 'obvious' shortlist and an internationally famous winner, another for excluding suitably experienced architects through its pre-selection process in favour of more local practices. In one case there were problems in implementing what some regarded as an innovative winning design, in another there was criticism that the promoter went for a safe but less imaginative option.

But in each of these competitions, the procedures were carefully thought through, professional advice was taken, the competitors were well briefed and the promoters made every effort to be fair both in how they operated their chosen system and in what they asked of competitors. All the procedures outlined in the following pages produced a winner and in every case the promoter was satisfied with the outcome. The earlier schemes have been built while the more recent ones are either in the process of being built or progressing through the design stages.

Case study 1 Sinderins sheltered housing, Dundee 1985

Introduction

Type of competition
A single-stage competition limited to architects under the age of 35, practising in Scotland.

Subject
A sheltered housing development for the elderly with warden cover.

Project value
The project value was approximately £730 000 at 1985 prices.

Promoter
The Scottish Special Housing Association (SSHA) in collaboration with the Royal Incorporation of Architects in Scotland.

Manager
The competition was managed by the RIAS.

Assessors
John Richards (then President of the RIAS): Architect Chairman
Robert Black: Architect
Harry Eccles: Regional Technical Manager, SSHA

Key points

The competition, held in 1985, just creeps into the decade on which this book is based. Because of the ten year gap, it has not been possible to give as detailed account of the competition procedure as in the more recent case studies which follow. The promoting body no longer exists (the SSHA was merged with Scottish Homes and the development was handed over to the Cleghorn Housing Association), some of the documentation is gone and the people involved have moved on. On the other hand, the timescale makes it possible to focus on a competition-winning scheme which has been both completed and tested in use over a number of years, and to assess how well the original objectives were met.

Few promoters would now follow the procedure outlined in 'Competition format' below. Most introduce additional checks and safeguards, such as 'pre-selection', interviews and some element of 'promoter choice'. This competition follows one of the simplest formats possible – a single stage with an outright winner, providing a base line against which the more complicated procedures can be measured. The fact that it worked (as did many others run to a similar format) demonstrates that competitions do not have to follow complex patterns.

The project won an RIBA Architecture Award (1990), and was commended in both the Civic Trust Awards and the Saltire Society Housing Design Awards (both 1990).

Background

The competition was launched by the Scottish Special Housing Association to celebrate the successful conclusion of its Festival of Architecture exhibition, 'A Mirror of Scottish Housing'. The site, which lies about a mile to the west of the centre of Dundee, was then owned by Dundee District Council and Tayside Regional Council. It had been cleared and grassed over by the Scottish Development Agency.

The site was situated on the corner of the Perth Road (a busy road close to shops and the bus route to the city centre) and a quieter cul-de-sac leading to a public car park. The surrounding area contained a mixture of differently scaled buildings, ranging from one to four storeys, with an existing four-storey tenement block adjacent to the new development on the main road.

The brief called for high quality accommodation with a 'non-institutional feel' while the District Council Planning Department required the development to 'make a major visual contribution to the street scene'. Space standards and cost requirements followed the housing association regulations current in Scotland at the time.

Approach

The promoters set themselves two objectives:

● to design and build a sheltered housing unit on a very important and visually sensitive site in the centre of Dundee, and
● to help set up or establish a young architectural practice.

The first objective was detailed in the brief (see below). To meet the second objective, the competition was opened to 'individual architects and firms, none of whose partners, directors or members will be above the age of 35 at 31 August 1985 [a date set at a few months after the result would be known] who practise in Scotland'.

Competition format

The format followed was that of the traditional architectural competition. The competition was open to all architects who fulfilled the eligibility requirements set out above. A brief was issued; written questions invited and answers circulated; and the designs submitted. The competitors were required to submit drawings (on no more than two A1 sheets) to include:

● Site plan and landscape proposals showing to a scale of 1:200, location of roads and services, relationships of buildings, points of particular interest, and landscaping.

- Floor plans, sections and elevations to a scale 1:100 sufficient to explain the design, and illustrate special relationships, circulation, massing, construction and servicing.
- Perspective, axonometric sketches or birds-eye views which illustrate the character and nature of the proposed buildings and show their relationships to the surrounding area. (This requirement was a discretionary one but the promoter asked competitors to make sure that drawings were included to 'adequately represent the proposals in any publication in the lay or technical press'.)

A technical committee 'representing the SSHA and other interested parties' examined the designs and checked that they met the requirements of the brief. A report was prepared for the assessors. On the basis of the material submitted and with reference to the technical report, the panel of assessors selected first, second and third prize winners. The promoter appointed the designers of the scheme placed first as the architects for the work. The whole process was conducted with total anonymity preserved throughout.

Brief

The brief was a compact document, supported by a number of detailed appendices. It gave outline information on the location (including adjacent buildings and facilities), roads and access, the site (plans, dimensions and ground conditions), and planning requirements. Printed sheets of photographs of the site and its immediate surroundings were included.

Competitors were required to provide 'a minimum of 25 and maximum of 35 units, including the warden's house'. The number was to be 'compatible with the requirements of the brief, the provision of a high standard living environment and a satisfactory relationship of the form of the buildings and layout to their surroundings'. (The winning architects were able to provide a total of 28 units.) Detailed information was given on the space standards to be met and the supporting facilities required. Competitors were also asked to consider circulation, access and servicing. (Provision was to be in accordance with general standards established by the SSHA for all such developments. These were detailed in the appendices.)

The brief also set out general aims such as the need for privacy, protection from noise, provision of views and the enjoyment of daylight wherever possible.

The appendixed documentation included:

- Soil investigation report.
- Detailed standards to be met in all SSHA developments.
- Sample layouts of houses and flats based on these standards (these were provided for guidance, competitors were not obliged to use any of the standard layouts).
- Indicative costs for public housing and methods of calculation.

A pro-forma was provided for competitors to list the provision made (e.g. how many units and of what type) and give costings.

A location plan, site plan (1:1250) and a site survey (1:200) were provided to all competitors. As the site was public open space and entry was unrestricted no arrangements were made for site visits.

Costs and prizes

Prizes of £3000, £1500 and £500 were offered, the first prize being an advance of the fees due to the architect on appointment.

No information on administrative, management and consultancy costs is available.

Timetable

Competition announced	December 1984
Last date for questions	25 January 1985
Answers circulated by	1 February 1985
Submission of entries	19 March 1985

Winner's approach

The architects picked up two key criteria from the brief: the need for a non-institutional approach and the need for the development to form an integral part of the local area.

Figure 11.1 *Sheltered housing, Sinderins, Dundee. Architects: Page and Park*

Their solution divides the accommodation into three distinct and separate units:

- fronting the Perth Road, a five-storey building provides flats on the four upper levels with service areas and shared facilties on the ground floor. It includes a common room at the corner of the development which gives views both to the street and garden areas. The building continues the line of the existing, adjacent tenement block, screening the rest of the development from the busy road.
- a two-storey unit, on a more residential scale, accommodating the requirement for some two-bedroom flats.
- a 'garden wall' unit, of three storeys, positioned to provide enclosure for the development as a whole.

The three separate units are positioned to provide both privacy and contact. They enclose garden areas with linking paths, protected from the exterior surroundings but overlooked by the residents themselves.

The exterior of the buildings relate to their locality in terms of both style and scale without resorting to pastiche. The use of pink and grey blockwork provides an individual identity for the development as a whole and acts as a visual link between the different elements.

The interior layout groups the flats into clusters with the individual front doors sharing a common landing. The architects also made an effort to introduce individuality into what was inevitably somewhat standard provision by introducing special features wherever possible, e.g. a balcony, a spectacular view, a quiet garden aspect.

Outcome

The project proceeded through the design stages and building stages and was completed in 1989. The development was featured in the *Architects' Journal* in May 1990, where the writer comments on the design background to the project as follows:

> A competition such as this is both a courageous step by a client who could have taken the more traditional route of choosing an experienced practice, and a tremendous opportunity for young practices to produce a quality solution that could give them their first major break . . . the built solution matches the competition drawings closely, which, according to the architect, was due to the brief being well conceived and the SSHA being an ideal client, providing great support and experience as the design developed.

He goes on to describe the building as a 'thoughtful and sensitive solution through an exquisitely crafted piece of architecture which also manages to be "homely and safe" and is extremely well received by wardens and residents alike'. Four years later, discussions with those currently responsible for the buildings, confirm that this is still the case.

Although the SSHA cannot be consulted, the praise and awards which the scheme has attracted would suggest that the first of the SSHA's objectives in promoting the competition was met. As far as the second objective is concerned, the Sinderins development was one of two significant competition wins and commissions which helped establish the Glasgow-based practice of Page and Park, the other being the Glasgow Cathedral Urban Design Competition. The latter, implemented in phases over a six year period, was recognised by five separate design award schemes.

Page and Park have built on these initial successes and established themselves as one of Scotland's leading design practices. Their subsequent work includes the Italian Centre, Glasgow; the Visitor Reception Centre, Brodick, Isle of Arran; the Hill House, Helensburgh; Strathclyde University Campus plan, Glasgow and St Mungo Museum, Glasgow.

Case study 2   Avenue de Chartres car park, Chichester 1989

Introduction

Type of competition
An open, single-stage, competition to produce a shortlist of three schemes from which the promoter selects the overall winner (promoter choice).

Subject
A multi-deck car park to accommodate a minimum of 900 cars situated at the key entrance point to the historic city of Chichester, West Sussex.

Project value
£6.9 million was allocated for the building and associated works (inclusive of all fees).

Promoter
Chichester District Council.

Manager
The RIBA Competitions Office.

Assessors
Four assessors were appointed, two nominated by the RIBA and two by the promoters. They were:

Sir William Whitfield CBE: Chairman and RIBA nominee
Professor Derek Lovejoy: RIBA nominee
Jake Stocker MVO: Chairman of the Public Services Committee, Chichester District Council
Roderick Fennell: Chief Technical Officer, Chichester District Council

The promoter also appointed James Hill (Structural Engineer) and Clive Sayer (Surveyor) as technical advisers to the panel to provide specific guidance.

Key points

Chichester had a growing parking problem which needed to be resolved in a manner compatible with the city's unique character. The site was seen as one 'which invites a new approach to the design of car parks in sensitive areas.' The promoter was looking for a scheme which would justify the quality of the site allocated to it and be recognised as a main entrance to the city rather than 'merely a necessary facility in a back-yard environment'.

Although the implementation of the scheme was not totally without problems, the competition was regarded as a success by the promoter and has frequently been cited as an example of the system working effectively. The winning group of young architects set up their own practice (Birds, Portchmouth and Russum) as a result of gaining this commission. The completed project has since won almost a record number of design awards (see 'Outcome' below).

Approach

Having established the amount of increased car parking required and approved a design brief drafted by its Technical Services Department, Chichester District Council agreed to promote an architectural competition 'to determine the practicality of constructing a high quality decked car park at the Avenue de Chartres site'. It appointed the RIBA to organise the competition and independent consultants to give technical advice on the design brief and the submissions.

The competition was organised in one stage only. This is unusual for a project of this size and complexity. The promoter gave the reason as one of simple expediency. At the time, it was anticipated that the government would place further restrictions on capital expenditure and that this might well prevent the scheme being implemented unless an early commitment was made. In the event, the single-stage format worked quite well, and achieved its objective in terms of timing. But the promoter agrees that a two-stage competition would probably have eased the implementation of the project both for the architects and the technical support team.

The 'promoter choice' format required the assessors to shortlist three schemes and report back to the Council, whose members would then select the winner of their choice. The competition conditions were drawn up by the RIBA and followed the standard requirements in all respects.

The competition conditions set out to encourage innovative thinking and the acceptance of car parks as a major new urban building type. To allow for varied and imaginative responses no specific building form was specified. Competitors were free to range from landscape solutions through to built forms, subject only to a satisfactory functional performance.

Competition format

The competition was open to all architects. Details of the competition were advertised in the technical press by the RIBA Competitions Office. Two hundred and twenty-one sets of documents were despatched and 85 entries submitted. The competition documents comprised the standard conditions, the development brief (giving the context for development), the design brief (setting out the design requirements), minimum performance specifications, a site plan and photographs of the site and its immediate surroundings.

Competitors were asked to provide the following drawings:

- Site plan (scale 1:500), using as a base the drawing provided.
- Ground plan (scale 1:200), showing overall character of the scheme at ground level. It was left to the competitors' discretion whether or not to show other levels. If they did these were to be drawn to the scale 1:500.
- Elevations and sections sufficient to explain the scheme.

- Typical elevation (scale 1:50) sufficient to show character and standard of detailing.
- Sketches or perspectives were permitted but not specifically required.

All drawings had to be contained on no more than nine A1 sheets and accompanied by a concise description of the design not exceeding eight sides of A4. No models were accepted. Each entry had to be accompanied by a capital cost analysis for which a pro-forma was included in the documentation.

On the advice of the assessors, it was decided that no opportunity would be given for competitors to ask questions or seek to clarify the brief. (The 'question and answer' procedures set out in the RIBA guidelines are presented as an option for promoters.) In this situation, the 'no question' decision endorsed the open approach established in the brief.

On the basis of the information submitted, the assessors selected three schemes and prepared a detailed report on each scheme. Technical reports were also prepared. The entire procedure was conducted without any knowledge of the identities of the entrants. (The two envelope system was used to preserve anonymity; see page 49).

The three shortlisted schemes were submitted by:

Andrew Birds, Richard Portchmouth and Michael Russum, London.
Manning, Clamp and Partners, Richmond, Surrey.
John Pardey and Ronald Yee Architects, London.

The three teams were invited to make a presentation, illustrated by plans and models, to a specially convened full day meeting of the Council's Public Services Committee. Each team was allocated half an hour in which to make the presentation and a further half hour in which to answer questions. The assessors attended the meeting in an advisory capacity. The public were excluded from the meeting for a short period while the assessors gave a confidential report outlining the strengths and weaknesses of each of the selected designs and commenting on the organisational capacities of the firms involved.

At the end of the full day session, the committee members voted on their choice of winner: Andrew Birds, Richard Portchmouth and Michael Russum. The winning scheme was favoured by a substantial majority (13 out of 16).

The client set up a strong team to work with the architects to bring the project to completion. The team included a project manager and a technical consultant with specialist experience in the design of multi-storey car parks. This additional expertise was brought in partly to support the young design team but also to ensure that the high standard sought by the competition could be achieved in its implementation. This meant that the consultancy fees were substantially higher than they would have been for a more routine project, although there was an element of fee negotiation, not provided for in the conditions, before the architects were appointed.

Brief and competitors' response

The competition brief was drawn up by the promoter and edited by the chairman of the panel of assessors. It set out the background to the proposed development and described the site, specifying the special conditions relating to its planning and development. Minimum performance specifications were given together with details of the amount of provision required. The aim was to achieve a design which married functional efficiency and aesthetic effect. The objectives set out in the brief were:

- the need to design a car park which would fit with the historic character of the area;
- the desire to learn from others' mistakes and not build a maintenance liability;
- the new car park should be user friendly, convenient and safe for pedestrians as well as drivers;
- value for money.

The assessors hoped to see 'a breakthrough in car park design'. What they got was 'an entry notable for the rich variety of solutions' though with no single scheme which fully answered their expectations.

> The imbalance between functional efficiency and aesthetic effort was generally present in many schemes and generated much discussion amongst assessors and not a little difficulty as well. Although we remain sure that these two aspects of design are not mutually exclusive, we accept that the problems of combining the two and responding as well to a sensitive site are truly daunting.
>
> (Assessors' report)

Most of the solutions offered fell into one of four types:

- **Walled enclosures:** a straightforward multi-storey structure within some form of walled enclosure.
- **Elevational treatments:** dependent on presenting a facade, screening the parking provision.
- **'High-tech' solutions:** several schemes were considered to be excellent for their kind but too visually competitive to be appropriate for this site.
- **Concealed buildings:** the assessors expected to see more schemes based primarily on earth-forming and landscaping. There were some entries which reached the final stage in the assessment procedure but they were eventually eliminated because of practical problems which had not been successfully resolved.

The three selected schemes were considered to be excellent in their overall design. Although each had some 'relatively minor shortcomings' the assessors considered that in each case adjustments could be made without disturbing the essential integrity of the solutions.

Costs and prizes

Prizes of £15 000, £7000 and £3000 were offered, the first being regarded as a payment on account of fees payable to the winner when engaged as architect to carry out the project.

The total cost of the competition itself was just under £18 000 with £4400 of this recouped from registration fees. Assessors' fees amounted to £3000 and the RIBA management fee accounted for a further £3000.

Timetable

Registration by	12 December 1988
Closing date for submissions	27 February 1989
Assessment and selection of three schemes	Mid-March 1989
Presentations and final selection	22 March 1989
Architect appointed	18 May 1989
Work started on site	28 December 1989
Completion date	10 March 1991

Winner's approach

The relationship of the car park to the Cathedral and medieval city wall inspires the design of a new city wall providing an elevated tree-lined pedestrian 'wall walk' along Avenue de Chartres into the heart of Chichester.

The wall walk screens the multi-deck car park and combines with the medieval city wall to form the new western approach to Chichester, creating a new city entrance portal as it bridges

Figure 11.2 *Avenue de Chartres car park, Chichester. Architects: Birds, Portchmouth and Russum*

Avenue de Chartres. Like the medieval wall encircling historic Chichester, the new city wall re-establishes the edge to the city.

Within the 900 space car park visitors can park directly alongside generous, well illuminated and brightly colour-coded pedestrian aisles which lead towards the circular stair towers and access to the wall walk at first-floor level.

Promoter's response

The Council was well aware that it was always going to be difficult to insert a decked car park successfully into a small historic city. Whilst, as the assessors noted, the competition did not achieve the quantum leap which the Council had originally sought, it did allow members to evaluate 85 different approaches and did produce a winning scheme which cleverly camouflaged the bulk of the car park and made a positive, modern architectural statement. The Council considers that the competition successfully demonstrated that it is possible to design car parks to a high standard – they do not have to be the Cinderella of the urban landscape, but can make a successful modern contribution which fulfils a valuable function while complementing a historic setting.

Outcome

The completed project is considered to have both its champions and its critics partly because Chichester has no other building like it. But then Chichester has no other building which has been showered with so many design awards: a Civic Trust award, two RIBA awards, a West Sussex County Council award, a lighting award and an English Tourist Board commendation. The breadth of the awards is seen as an immense credit to the imagination and skill of the architects and ample justification for what the District Council still regards as its 'brave' decision to build the competition-winning scheme.

Case study 3   The Museum of Scotland, Edinburgh 1991

Introduction

Type of competition
A two-stage international competition with an interview-based shortlisting procedure introduced between the first and second stages. The final selection was made by the promoter.

Subject
The design of a new building adjacent to and linking with the Royal Museum of Scotland, Chambers Street, Edinburgh – to provide display space for the Scottish collections of the National Museums of Scotland (NMS).

Project value
The building construction (government funded) cost was set at £22 million excluding VAT and professional fees. A further £5 million was to be raised from the private sector for fitting out the completed building (1989 prices).

Promoter
The Board of Trustees of the National Museums of Scotland.

Manager
The Royal Incorporation of Architects in Scotland (RIAS) Competitions Office.

Assessors
Sir Philip Dowson: Architect and Jury Chairman
The Marquess of Bute: Chairman of the Board of Trustees, National Museums of Scotland
Professor Peter Jones: Trustee, National Museums of Scotland
The Earl of Perth: Chairman of the National Museums of Scotland Patrons' Organisation
Dr Robert Anderson: Director, National Museums of Scotland
Professor Hans Hollein: Architect
Miss Eva Jiricna: Architect
Professor Andrew MacMillan: Architect

Key points

A great deal of care was taken throughout the initial stages of this project. This was reflected in the quality of the briefing offered to competitors and in the comparative ease with which it has proceeded through its various stages.

One of the most important steps in the process of obtaining support for the project was the commissioning of a feasibility study. It was undertaken by a team led by architect John Richards, and set out to establish detailed requirements in terms of space and facilities; test and demonstrate the practicability of placing the building on the Chambers Street site; and work out what the overall costs were likely to be. This involved the team in the design of a 'test' building, complete with a block model. The work carried out for this study provided the basis for the competition brief. It also established cost estimates which enabled the NMS to secure funding for the project before the competition itself was launched.

When the decision to hold a competition was announced, the NMS Board of Trustees held a symposium to present and explain their whole approach to the project. Speakers included The Marquess of Bute, Chairman of the Trustees; John Spencely, President of the RIAS; and Sir Philip Dowson, the Senior Assessor as well as John Walsh, Director of the J Paul Getty Museum in California; Robert Anderson, NMS Director; and Marina Vaizey, Art Critic of the *Sunday Times*. They outlined the background to the project, the research which had been undertaken, the aims and objectives of the competition, the key points of the brief, and the museum context in which they were all working. The seminar was recorded and its proceedings were subsequently published. Each competitor received a copy of the publication as part of the briefing pack.

Although this was an international competition it did not follow the requirements set down by the International Union of Architects (IUA). In fact, the IUA issued a press notice dissociating itself from the competition on the grounds that it contravened its regulations in several respects: the composition of the jury; anonymity requirements; 'promoter choice' elements and the commitment to exhibit only second-stage entries. (The criticism of the jury may seem puzzling. Two of the architects were 'international' in the sense that they were not UK nationals but they both had very strong associations with the country. The inclusion of an English element in a Scottish competition was not regarded as fulfilling IUA 'international' requirements.)

The decision not to go through the IUA was a deliberate one, made on the advice of the RIAS. Several of the procedures considered to be appropriate for this project would have been precluded if IUA rules had been followed.

Background

The promise of government funding for the project was achieved as the result of a long campaign. It was agreed as early as 1951 that a new museum would be provided, but it was not until the 1980s that any firm progress was made. To secure funding, the trustees had to demonstrate not only the feasibility of a building on the Chambers Street site but also its financial and functional superiority to possible alternatives in other parts of Scotland. The campaign culminated in an exhibition 'The Wealth of a Nation' (1989) which demonstrated the range and quality of material available for permanent display. In January 1990 the Secretary of State for Scotland finally agreed to fund the project on the Chambers Street site.

Approach

In his introduction to the seminar, The Marquess of Bute describes the creation of a National Museum as:

A cherished hope of Scottish people. It is much more than purely a museum adventure, it is something which is important to the community and to our Nation. The overriding imperative is that what we create for Scotland should be something of remark and of excellence: we cannot tolerate the second rate or the cheap or the average.

The trustees saw their role as one of patron and the competition route as the most acceptable way of selecting an architect for a project of this significance.

Scotland has for many years had a stronger tradition of competitions than many other parts of the UK and the RIAS has taken an active role in promoting the system. It was, therefore, taken as self-evident that the RIAS should assist with the organisation of such an important national project.

Competition format

The format was quite a complicated one in terms of the selection stages and procedures used. The aim was to reduce the numbers involved in preparing design work while ensuring that all competitors were capable of carrying out the job. Five hundred and sixty architects responded to the advertisement of the competition. (Each one paid £125 for a copy of the briefing pack.) Three hundred and seventy-one entries were received. The promoters wished to keep the requirements for the first stage to a minimum and competitors were simply asked to submit two A1 boards and a short text to explain their design ideas. The aim was to encourage entries from the widest range of talent by minimising the technical requirements at the first stage. (Competitors in the second stage were to be paid a fee and the thought was that less experienced teams would therefore be able to bring in additional support.)

The assessors reduced consideration of the first stage entries to 51 after their first day's assessment. By the end of the second day twelve entries had been shortlisted for interview. The entry envelopes were then opened to reveal the identity of the entrants and the shortlist of twelve were invited for interview by the assessors. The purpose of the interview stage was twofold:

● to allow the assessors an opportunity to question the entrants on their design approach; and
● to assess their capability of carrying out the project.

Assessments were undertaken by a number of bodies including the Royal Fine Art Commission for Scotland; representatives of the planning and highways authorities; in addition a team of consultant building professionals appointed by the museum and the museum's own curatorial and technical staff formed a technical assessment panel. Reports from all these assessments were made available to the Committee of Assessors at the start of their second-stage assessment.

Six teams were invited to proceed to the second stage of the competition. Supplementary briefing information was issued (dealing in the main with the display of exhibition material), and a briefing meeting held for all second-stage competitors.

At this stage, competitors were required to prepare a 'design scheme', in accordance with the full brief. They were asked to submit:

- eight A1 drawings, showing plans, sections and elevations to 1:200 scale and perspectives;
- one A1 sheet showing technical aspects of the design;
- two A1 sheets illustrating the design approach which would be adopted for displays of different kinds of museum objects;
- one further A1 sheet to be used at the competitor's discretion;
- a written report covering technical performance (general, structure and materials, services and environmental control);
- a summary cost report (to a supplied format);
- a 1:200 model (a template was provided for the construction of the model so that it would fit into a base model of the surrounding area constructed by the National Museum of Scotland).

The original conditions required plans, elevations and sections be drawn to a smaller scale (1:200). This was subsequently changed to 1:500 (with the limit on the number of A1 sheets raised to accommodate this) and the requirement for a model was introduced. The changes in scale and model were introduced because it became evident, from the material submitted in the first stage, that more detail was essential to judge the design proposals. These changes were agreed with each of the competitors (on a form which they signed). The prizes and honoraria were increased to compensate for the extra costs incurred by competitors.

Before the assessment panel met, all the material was submitted to a panel of technical advisers. They prepared a written report on each entry for the assessors.

The Committee of Assessors reported 'the outcome of its deliberations' to the Board of Trustees who had undertaken to 'proceed with the appointment of an architect for the project taking full account of the recommendations of the assessors'.

Brief

The brief was a straightforward and compact document containing a range of information within its 16 pages of text. It began by stating the key objectives in relation to display spaces; quality of design and buildings; and the relationships with the existing building and surrounding area. The first stage was judged on the competitors' approach to these three objectives.

The brief set out cost guidelines and site details. It also gave guidance on highways and access and on planning considerations. These had been discussed with the relevant authorities and the information given in the brief was endorsed by them.

A further section of the brief detailed the project requirements in terms of primary function and spatial dimensions. The environmental conditions to be provided in the display areas were given as a general standard to be met – not detailed for specific items at this stage.

The overall approach to display is set out in terms of the main groupings and more detailed information is given on specific items which have to be accommodated (e.g. the Hilton of Cadboll Stone, weighing 7 tonnes; the Rossend painted ceiling, dimensions 8.53 $\times$ 6.1 metres; and the Boulton and Watt steam engine, 25 tonnes in weight and producing noise and vibration in motion).

The briefing documentation included:

- plans, sections and elevations of the Royal Museum of Scotland and the adjacent Museum of Scotland site. (The new museum was to link in with the existing building);
- 'The Wealth of a Nation' – 1989 publication illustrating the Scottish Collections of the National Museums of Scotland;
- 'A New Museum for Scotland' proceedings of the symposium held to launch the competition;
- photographs of the site, the existing buildings and the surrounding area;
- additional photographs of items in the NMS Collections.

More detailed information on display philosophy and requirements was circulated at the second stage.

Costs and prizes

A prize fund of £40 000 was made available to the assessors to distribute amongst the projects placed first, second and third and payments of £9500 were awarded to each of the remaining second-stage competitors.

The total cost to the NMS of running the competition was £195 000. This included all printing and distribution costs, fees, prize awards and the cost of an exhibition after the competition result had been announced. These costs were partly offset by the entry fees paid by competitors.

Timetable

Competition symposium	16 October 1990
Funding confirmed	January 1990
Competition launched	14 January 1991
First-stage submissions by	15 April 1991
Assessment panel meeting and interviews	13–15 May 1991
Shortlist announced	16 May 1991
Second-stage briefing	17 May 1991
Second-stage submissions by	19 July 1991
Result and exhibition	August 1991

Winner's approach

The winning architects, Benson + Forsyth, describe their building as both reflecting the past – 'the language of the building draws extensively on the traditional architecture of Scotland' – and looking to the future – 'a building of our time, hinging on the twenty-first century'. The design has been described as 'strikingly modern' complementing the neighbouring Royal Museum while bringing a new element into the 'sedate' Chambers Street.

Figure 11.3 *Museum of Scotland model. Architects: Benson + Forsyth*

It features a high fortress style front wall and an imposing corner tower which the architects see as the 'locating symbol' for the museum. The rooftop hanging garden provides a visual contrast, relating the museum to the city and the landscape.

The interior provides a range of exhibition and display areas each with its individual characteristics.

Promoter's response

Viewed from the museum's perspective, the competition was successful in several important areas:

- in helping the NMS to define its requirements
- in engaging the input of experienced external advisors
- in helping to publicise and gain suport for the project, its aims and purposes
- in identifying architects and an architectural approach well suited to the project.

Overall the NMS regards the competition as having been very worthwhile and good value for money. It did, however, find that the competition process was time-consuming, relatively costly and demanding in terms of administrative and management input.

Outcome

The outcome in terms of the selection of Benson + Forsyth as architects for the project and the design approach adopted in their scheme met the museum's objectives for the project; in Lord Bute's words to produce 'something of remark and excellence' to house Scotland's national collections of natural science, history and technology.

The architectural integration of the functional requirements of the building with the exhibitions it contains and the relationship of the building to the special urban context of the city of Edinburgh all appear likely to be successfully addressed by the detailed designs developed from the competition scheme.

Work started on site in May 1993 and the museum is scheduled to open in August 1998.

Case study 4   The Richard Attenborough Centre for Disability and the Arts, University of Leicester 1993

Introduction

Type of competition
A two-stage open competition organised to the traditional first, second and third prize format.

Subject
A new Arts Centre for people with disabilities on a site adjacent to the University of Leicester. The Centre is to provide a specialist teaching and research base in the field of disability and the arts and is to offer a broad curriculum including the visual arts, music, drama and theatre.

Project value
The budget for the actual building (excluding site aquisition, demolition costs, fees, furniture and fittings and VAT) was £865 000.

Promoter
The competition was promoted by the University of Leicester through the Richard Attenborough Centre for Disability and the Arts and sponsored by the *Independent*. The Centre is part of the Department of Adult Education at the University of Leicester.

Manager
The RIBA was appointed to manage the competition.

Assessors
The assessment panel comprised two architect assessors nominated by the RIBA, and two nominees of the promoter. Lord Attenborough, Chairman of Access and Jonathan Glancey, Architectural Correspondent of the *Independent* joined the assessment team in an advisory capacity. The assessors were:

Peter Randall: RIBA Senior Assessor
Maxwell Hutchinson: RIBA Second Assessor
Dr K J R Edwards: Vice Chancellor, Leicester University
Dr Eleanor Hartley: Director, Richard Attenborough Centre

The technical advisory team comprised the University's Estates and Services Bursar, Richard Float; disabled groups; the local Access officer and specific professional performers with disabilities.

Key points

The objective of the competition was to seek ideas which challenge current thought about designing for disabled people. The promoter was looking for a building 'with unique qualities which would address the issues of disability through the language of architecture'.

The University Estates Office, together with the staff and students of the Centre, were involved in drawing up the brief. After the selection of the six finalists, there was a period of consultation with disabled people and their representative organisations who commented on the drawings and about design points in general. These comments were incorporated into the additional guidance notes (see 'Brief' below). The process of consultation with disabled people continued throughout the competition. The client describes this as 'a hall-mark of the winning architect's refinements at scheme design'.

Interviews were introduced between the first and second stages. Although this did not affect the outcome of the competition (the winner was selected on the basis of the submitted material), it was seen as a vital part of the process enabling the promoter and the architects to discuss their ideas and expectations before the more detailed design work was undertaken. It also served to reassure the promoters that they could work with any of the teams selected from the first stage.

Background

The Centre was founded in 1982 and initially provided sculpture classes for people with visual impairment. Its activities broadened to include the arts generally and to embrace other types of disability. It became a research centre with emphasis on the broad dissemination of its knowledge of teaching arts to people with disabilities. The original Centre occupied premises comprising various rooms and offices across the Leicester University campus: a situation which the able bodied found inconvenient and which presented additional problems of access and orientation to those users with some form of disability.

A site was acquired, adjacent to the University and fundraising started for a purpose-built centre.

Approach

The Centre saw an opportunity to focus attention on 'best practice' solutions to designing for those with disabilities. The proposal to hold a competition was put forward by the Centre's Patron, Sir Richard Attenborough, supported by a group of Honorary Patrons who considered that it would both further the Centre's key objectives and help raise the funds necessary to complete the building. In response to an approach by Sir Richard Attenborough, the *Independent* agreed to sponsor the competition, providing publicity and contributing towards the running costs.

The site for the new building, though well-located, was not a particularly stimulating one. The new Centre would be overshadowed by two adjacent large modern buildings and so needed to make its own statement. The promoters were looking for a solution which would be inviting; provide a stimulating environment in which to work and which would be seen as 'life enhancing'.

Competition format

The competition was open to all UK-registered architects. There was an entry fee of £29.38 (£25 plus 17.5% VAT). Three hundred and five architects responded to the competition invitation and 128 submitted entries.

In the first stage competitors were required to submit no more than two A1 sized sheets which could contain 'any material which the competitors feel will present their proposals in the most persuasive way' but had to include:

- a site plan (scale 1:500);
- floor plans and sections (scale 1:100);
- a perspective sketch (from a given viewpoint);
- a detailed layout (scale 1:50) of a portion of the building, including the foyer, to demonstrate how the needs of the disabled would be met.

A two-page report and simple cost analysis 'sufficient to assist the assessors in determining whether cost targets are being met' were also to be submitted.

At this stage the assessors were looking for 'an outline design to illustrate the concept, bearing in mind the site constraints and need to provide a suitable image for the Centre'. Additional criteria required the solutions to be 'practical and economic' and competitors to demonstrate a knowledge of and feeling for the needs of disabled people.

Six schemes were selected 'where potentially the building would fit well into the context'. They were submitted by:

- Roger Hawkins, Lucy Montgomery and Andy Gollifer
- Honor Thomson, Simon Usher and Dorian Wiszniewski
- Robert Doe and Kut Nadiadi
- Hook Whitehead Stanway
- Summerlin Payne Architects
- Ian E Taylor

Some were fully worked out. Others were rather more sketchy but included on the basis of the assessors' 'appreciation of the general concept'. The authors of the shortlisted schemes were each invited to an interview with representatives of the client body (including the Patron and the Vice-Chancellor) advised by the Senior Assessor. This was an unusual procedure for an RIBA competition (although it may become more general in the future) and was organised at the insistence of the promoter who wanted to be sure that they could work with any of the potential architects. The nature of the project required someone who had a clear idea of what they wanted to do but were receptive, open-minded and adaptable. On this basis, all six shortlisted competitors were accepted to proceed to the second stage. The interviews were also used as an additional briefing process. The promoter ensured that certain specified information was given to each team. This interview stage was seen as essential by the client: 'This was a key process in making our final decisions.' Interestingly, an attempt was made to preserve anonymity throughout the interview process – the architects were referred to only as A, B, C, etc. The client comments, 'We tried to black out any clues as to identity and concentrate on the issues in hand.

It was a very intense experience with the discussions continuing throughout the whole day.'

Additional guidance notes were prepared and circulated to all the second-stage competitors to supplement the information given in the brief. Much of the guidance focussed on the primary function of the building. Competitors were reminded that 'this is not a day-centre but a purpose built arts centre for everyone's use'. The promoters stressed the need for clear, easy to understand, circulation for all: 'Tactile maps should be an added luxury not a necessity!' and found it necessary to remind competitors of the importance of 'referring to the bibliography of the original brief'. Most of the notes refer to general points. A few specific points are made (e.g. 'scheme 104 has inadequate toilet provision') but all the information was circulated to all second-stage competitors. Each of the second-stage competitors were invited to visit the Centre and talk to the students.

The second-stage submission requirements were as follows:

- perspective drawings and/or strip elevations showing the building in context;
- a site plan (scale 1:100) showing external spaces, landscape, surfaces, footpaths and access ramps, etc.;
- floor plans and sections, scale 1:50 (1:100 also permitted);
- detailed layouts of a portion of the building, including the gallery/hall with full annotation at 1:50 or larger;
- a detailed report on not more than ten A4 sheets. This was to include an elemental breakdown of costs and detailed comment on energy consumption.

Competitors were asked to annotate their drawings 'to demonstrate their understanding of and special provision for people with disabilities'.

The final selection was made on the basis of the material submitted. Ian E Taylor was awarded first prize with Roger Hawkins, Lucy Montgomery and Andy Gollifer coming second and Honor Thomson, Simon Usher and Dorian Wiszniewski being placed third.

Brief

The same basic brief was used for both stages of the competition, drawn up in consultation with the Senior Assessor. An additional explanatory document was circulated to all second-stage competitors drawing attention to important aspects of the initial brief.

After an initial introduction outlining the background to the project, the brief opened with a statement of key criteria. It went on to set out details of the site and planning requirements. Outline planning permission had already been obtained by the University Estates Office and a summary of its conditions was included in the brief. The Local Authority requested that no competitors contact them during Stage 1 of the competition.

A schedule of accommodation was given listing spaces and specifying uses, special requirements and desirable relationships between spaces but only defining sizes for smaller rooms such as the offices (e.g. Sculpture Studio. This will be the largest of three working spaces and will be adequate for 18–20 people generally with a maximum of 25).

Competitors were sent copies of the fund-raising brochure which set out the aims and activities of the Centre and a short bibliography was included in the brief. The following information was also provided:

- 6 photographs of the site and its immediate surroundings;
- a site survey (scale 1:100);
- drawings of the adjacent buildings;
- site plan showing adjacent sites;
- section through the nearby road;
- ordnance extract.

The brief was drawn up in sufficient detail to serve both stages but guidance notes were prepared between the first and second stages drawing attention to criteria which assessors felt had not been fully met by all second-stage schemes. These related in the main to:

- internal circulation, turning spaces, passing points, means of escape, size of lifts, WC access, etc.
- 'feel': e.g. 'A light and airy ambience is to be encouraged.'
- positioning of key spaces: e.g. 'It is doubtful that the promoters will be able to consider a final design featuring a first-floor hall/gallery.'

Costs and prizes

Prizes of £6000, £2000 and £1500 were offered with honoraria of £1000 being paid to each of the remaining second-stage competitors.

Timetable

Launch	5 May 1993
Receipt of questions	26 May 1993
Answers to questions	9 June 1993
First-stage submissions by	4 August 1993
Assessment and selection	week starting 23 August 1993
Second-stage brief issued	8 September 1993
Second-stage submissions	16 November 1993
Architect appointed	April 1994
Planning permission obtained	25 October 1994

Winner's approach

The winning team offers a solution which places an emphasis on simplicity of form and ease of construction throughout. The objective is to provide a framework strong enough to establish the overall form but with the flexibility to respond to the client's requirements as they develop during the design process.

Figure 11.4 *Model of the Centre. Architects: Ian E Taylor with Bennetts Associates. Model by Robert Kirkman*

The resulting design is an elegant composition of wall and glass. The building contains thick blockwork walls for space enclosure and sub-division, to provide thermal mass and insulation. The glazed areas take advantage of views over playing fields or open the interior to views of the sky, creating both optimum natural lighting and a sense of space.

The central roof light and 'shading' feature becomes the beacon for the Centre. In day it is lit by the sky, at night and in dull weather it is lit from below.

The design of the interior aims to provide natural clues to aid orientation and circulation within the building. This is achieved through strongly defined circulation routes and variation in the size and shape of spaces and in the materials used. The design seeks to encourage interaction (by providing informal meeting places and views from one area to another) as well as offering privacy when it is required.

Promoter's response

The winning design meets all our requirements and has provided something more. The new Centre will have a strong and elegant presence. It is a building of today which will hold its place with dignity, energy and optimism next to the giant edifices which surround it. It will have its own distinctive character and presence in the city.

Inside the design is eloquent and simple. There is no wasted space, no long corridors; the circulation encourages an amiable spirit in a living building. The clarity of direction gives ease of access for everyone.

The alchemy of space, people and resources will, we believe, promote a vibrant working environment in which the vision of the Centre will flourish.

(Extracts taken from the brochure accompanying the exhibition of the winning and other second-stage designs.)

Outcome

Work is scheduled to start on site during 1995 and the building should be completed in 1996.

Case study 5   Chalkhill estate, North Wembley, London 1993

This case study is taken from a report written by David Rock, who acted as adviser throughout the whole competition process and chaired the jury panel.

Introduction

Type of competition
A two-stage procedure designed to select a multi-disciplinary design and development team. The second stage was formulated to allow extensive consultation between the client officers, jury, residents and shortlisted teams.

Subject
The regeneration, by redevelopment, adaptation or renovation, of a 34-hectare late 1960s housing estate homes at North Wembley in the London Borough of Brent. One part of the estate comprises 30 six- and eight-storey blocks, housing a total of 1200 flats, while another part consists of 600 homes in traditionally built houses and three-storey flats in potentially pleasant, green layouts. The taller blocks are system built with the individual flats opening off deck access 'streets'. Other facilities on the site include schools, a health centre and a variety of community clubs.

The Chalkhill estate is excellently located near comprehensive shopping and urban facilities, and a London Undergound station just two stops from Baker Street.

Promoter
The London Borough of Brent initiated and organised the competition process.

Key points

The follow points deserve emphasis:

1. A project manager, a London Borough of Brent senior officer, was appointed from the outset to oversee the competition. The considerable delegation of authority within the client body meant that this officer was able to perform proactively and positively.
2. The client's commitment to the project in allocating considerable fees and prize money (£150 000 in total) to the shortlisted teams.
3. A uniquely 'open' three month process of continuous consultation between the jury; the five shortlisted teams; and residents, school and health centre leaders; planners; police; and many others.
4. The range of factors brought into the competition process. These included the planning context; urban design; funding and finance; building and infrastructure

costs; tenant and resident involvement with consultation at all stages; and job generation and training.
5. Collaborative working by the five teams to extend the brief during the second competition stage.

Background

The estate had been classified as 'hard to let' with a high proportion of people either unemployed or on housing benefit. Its reputation and image led to discrimination against those who lived there and made other people fearful of visiting. Despite this, people liked their homes internally (because of good space standards) and many of the older tenants had developed a great loyalty to the estate.

A strong resident involvement within Chalkhill had been built up but splits within its organisation and the tendency for the various ethnic communities to form their own groups had made consultation difficult.

Since Brent Council did not itself have access to all the necessary large financial resources for a major regeneration of the estate, it needed to find a team to bring the required expertise and private finance to the project. The competition route was chosen because it was considered likely that it would both maximise the input of private finance and bring different strategies, ideas and designs to bear on the problems involved.

Because of money already spent on the estate, the Department of the Environment required a full Options Appraisal to be undertaken before further bids could be considered. This involved a whole range of issues including design, employment, training, tenure mix, income generation and private sector finance, security and space standards, how to reduce communal areas and increase energy efficiency – all to be developed in the context of full resident participation.

A further factor was the advent of the government's Single Regeneration Budget (SRB), which offered the only likely source for the public monies share which the project needed. The SRB requirements echoed those of the DoE's Options Appraisal.

Approach

A Client Panel of resident representatives, Council officers and others met regularly from September 1992 to agree how the Options Appraisal should proceed. The Panel decided that a competition would be held and that a seven member jury should be appointed comprising three residents representatives, three Council Officers and an independent chairperson. After extensive consultation, architect David Rock was selected and appointed by Brent Council. His role, as well as chairing the jury meetings, was to act as adviser throughout the process; chair public meetings; help prepare the brief; write reports; and publicise the process.

Competition format
Initial invitation

The initial invitation process followed the EC directives with an advertisement placed in the *EC Journal* for 'organisations such as architects, developers, financial institutions and housing associations, or combinations thereof'. Advertisements were also placed in the national and trade press. These gave a short but succinct statement about the estate and a summary of the project's context. Applicants were invited to submit 'expressions of interest' to the Council so that they could be sent more detailed information. They were then asked to send information on their experience, skills and achievements under a number of appropriate and directional headings. Two hundred and ninety-five initial responses were received but the requirement to list completed housing schemes of over £1 m and other significant factors reduced the number of actual submissions to 37 including some from Italy, Denmark and France.

Stage 1 of the competition

The aim at this stage was to bring to the competition an imaginative mix and balance of different types of organisation, experience, approach and style. The 37 firms had been specifically asked, in making their submissions, not to address any of the requirements of what would become a large and diverse brief, but rather to demonstrate experience and excellence in past performance in significant comparable schemes. The jury was seeking to secure teams demonstrating exceptional qualities in each of the following key criteria:

- relevance of experience and solutions;
- design creativity;
- resident involvement and satisfaction;
- financial strength and inventiveness.

Other criteria considered were:

- employment generation;
- team character;
- presentation and clarity.

Three phases of marking were used to select the shortlist.

1. Each juror made the decision of In, Consider or Out. Collectively this reduced the number to 19.
2. These 19 were evaluated more formally, team by team, with the jury working together assessing against the seven criteria listed above. On this basis, seven teams went through to the final phase of marking.
3. The whole procedure was repeated until two of the schemes were finally rejected: one developer-led approach which scored lower marks than others of a similar nature and one which lacked the spark of excellence present in the shortlisted five.

A jury report was published and sent to all 37 original entrants. It gave the composition of every team; the jury's marking tables for each of the three phases; and a comment on each of the 37 submissions. Many entrants wrote to compliment Brent on this unusual but welcome decision to supply such detailed feedback at this stage.

The five teams chosen for the shortlist were:

1. Wimpey Group
   with
   Levitt Bernstein
   Metropolitan Housing Trust
   Capital Action
   Tenant Action
   Civic Trust Regeneration Unit

   Developers and contractors

   Architects
   Housing association
   Development consultancy
   Tenant friend organisation
   Employment and Training

2. AMEC Group
   with
   PRP Triangle
   Ealing Family HA
   Moorehead
   Dearle & Henderson
   Hillier Parker
   Roger Griffith Associates*
   Mark FitzPatrick*

   Developers and contractors

   Architects
   Housing association
   Consulting engineers
   Cost consultancy
   Development consultancy
   Landscape architects
   Employment and training

3. Burrell Foley Fischer
   with
   Bernard Williams Associates
   Dome
   Roger Tym & Partners
   Lovell Partnership*
   Colin Toms & Partners*
   Rybka Smith Ginsler & Battle*
   Victor Hausner & Associates*
   Paddington Churches HA*

   Architects

   Cost consultants
   Tenant friend organisation
   Town planning and economic development
   Developer and contractor
   Structural engineers
   Services and infrastructure consultants
   Development consultants
   Housing association

4. C.F. Moller Architects

   with
   Avanti Architects
   Turner and Townsend
   Unit for Architectural Studies
   Michael Jenkins
   Laing Homes*
   St George*
   Peabody Trust*
   Nationwide partners*

   Architects (a Danish firm bringing a European dimension to the competition)

   Architects
   Project management and quantity surveyors
   Urban special design
   Funding consultants
   Development and employment
   Development partners
   Housing association
   Housing trust and development

5. Shepheard Epstein & Hunter
   with
   Merlion Social Housing
   Gardiner and Theobald
   CPL Property Finance Brokers
   Chase Tyler*
   Royal Bank of Scotland*
   Trowers & Hamlins*

   Architects

   Enablers and development consultants
   Project manager and cost consultants
   Financial advisers
   Employment and training
   Funding
   Solicitors and legal advisers

(*added during Stage 2 of the competitition)

Stage 2 of the competition

After the brief was issued to the five teams, each team met the jury for a question and answer session. Then followed a three month period of continuous consultation between jury, teams, residents and others in the area:

- Initially the teams worked with each other and with the jury to understand and extend the brief.
- The Design Contest Office opened on the estate as a listening post, staffed by one team and tenant jurors on each weekday.
- A sketch model of the existing estate was built in this office by a member of the AMEC team
- A resident survey was arranged. A questionnaire was jointly drafted by the teams, in which the Moller team played a leading role. Fifty households were allocated to each team.
- The results were analysed by the Wimpey team, and superbly produced as wallcharts in time for the Options Weekend.
- The Options Weekend took place at the Cofers Community Centre on the estate with all teams, crime prevention and Council 'stalls'. Special events were organised to attract particular groups of residents.
- The jury chairman visited each team several times during the scheme presentations to discuss, in strict confidence, their design and funding proposals.
- Meetings took place between the chairman and teams together to co-ordinate the size and range of the submission material appropriate to the emerging solution.

The final submissions consisted of 10 to 16 A1 exhibition boards of drawings and other information; an options appraisal report; a scheme report covering details of concept, design, resident involvement, building costs, job generation, phase layout and design in greater detail; and a separate funding and financial report (kept confidential if so required).

After a half-day presentation to the jury and invited community 'observers' by each of the five teams, these final submissions went on public exhibition for two months, during which time the jury consulted all appropriate organisations and resident groups. Specialist meetings were held between the jury and each team to discuss their financial proposals in detail. Further mini-presentations were arranged for residents.

A final week-long jury session selected the winning strategy and team. Each submission was judged against seven criteria weighted as follows:

Concept and strategy	20%
Design quality	20%
Resident involvement and satisfaction	10%
Employment and training generation	5%
Quality of Phase 1 proposals	15%
Clarity and quality of presentation	5%
Finance	25%

The competing teams had strengths across the whole range. The jury evaluated each factor in great detail, with up to twenty criteria for each one. It was agreed from the start that mathematics would not, however, be the deciding factor but the long intensive marking process ensured a thorough understanding of each submission and was especially welcome to the lay members of the jury. Only 11% separated the five teams at this stage.

Overriding factors were then applied, including the acceptability of the strategy to the government, financial institutions and other stakeholders, tenant choice, numbers of homes produced, mix and type of rented dwellings and, crucially, the robustness and flexibility of the strategy to cope with changing design and financial requirements. These factors easily sorted out the winner from the other top teams.

The Brief

The additive nature of the briefing process has already been explained. This was based on an extremely detailed brief consisting of:

- general briefing notes including a contacts list, rules and timetable;
- outline brief and estate synopsis with plans, maps, drawings and dwellings information;
- guidance on Council housing strategy;
- statements by resident representatives, senior and local management, technical officers and the police;
- housing management information;
- information on special needs dwellings;
- schedules of capital expenditure and planned maintenance;
- structural and service engineer reports;
- details of security arrangements, concierge systems and car parking;
- the 1991 Census: estate extract and the 1992 Resident Survey results;
- minutes and reports of relevant committee and consultative meetings;
- estate newsletters and a history of published estate issues.

Timetable

Client panel plans project	September 1992
EC Journal advertisement	27 July 1993
Selection of the five Stage 2 contestants	24 September 1993
Detailed brief issued	8 November 1993
Question and answer sessions	15/16 November 1993
Open weekend	10–12 December 1993
Final submissions	7 February 1994
Presentations to jury	10–18 February 1994
Exhibition and consultation meetings	18 February–11 March 1994
Jury meetings	14 March–25 March 1994
Final jury session	28–31 March 1994
Announcement and presentation	8 April 1994

Costs

The total costs to the promoting body were just under £300 000 which were made up as follows:

- Honoraria
  (£20 000 to each of the five teams)   £100 000
- Winning team prize   £50 000
- Promoter's expenses
  (documentation, exhibitions, staff salaries and overheads, costs of
  the extensive consultative process)   £120 000
- Chairman and jury fees and expenses   £25 000

It is reported that the costs for each of the five teams ranged from £120 000 to £170 000.

Jury members

Chairman   David Rock (Architect)

Tenant representives   Akua Abban
(Elected after Stage 1)   Rita Gilmour
                            Grace Morris

Promoter's representatives (London Borough of Brent Housing Services)
John Garrity, Director of Commissioning
Gary Chase, Accountant (for Stage 1)
Jeff Zitron, HACAS (replacing Gary Chase for Stage 2)
George Varughese, Tenant Initiatives Manager
Derek Joseph, HACAS, deputised for Jeff Zitron in Stage 1.
Trevor Coulter, Chalkhill Project Manager from Brent Housing Services, partipated in all jury sessions as a non-voting member.

Winner's approach

The winning team, led by the Wimpey Group, was one of the four teams that opted for a new-build strategy, demolishing all 1200 deck access flats. Houses and low rise flats were planned around a series of streets, boulevards, courtyards, crescents and other varied patterns, with many non-housing activities. The open space, security, parking, phasing and many other planning factors were sensibly solved.

The financial package was particularly innovative, and called on many funding sources, with £75 m of the £95.3 m total package coming from private funds. The scheme produced 1027 low-rise homes for rent and 208 for shared ownership (compared with an average of 600 and 90 respectively on the other schemes). Foyer accommodation, medical centre, training and access centre, sheltered housing and a large park will also be affordable.

The jury recommended that, where possible, certain strategies selected from some of the other finalists should be considered by the winning team.

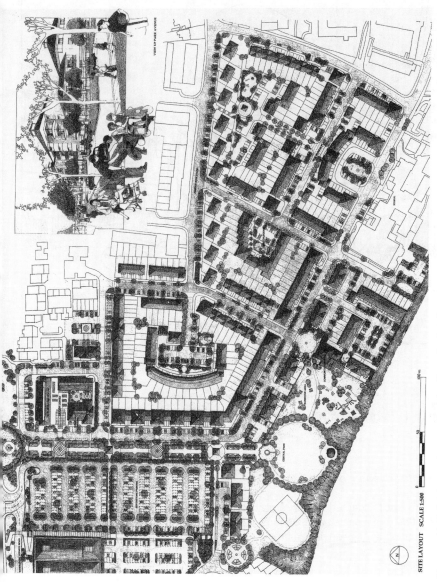

VIEW UP PARK AVENUE

SITE LAYOUT   SCALE 1:500

Figure 11.5 (a) Layout proposed by the winning team

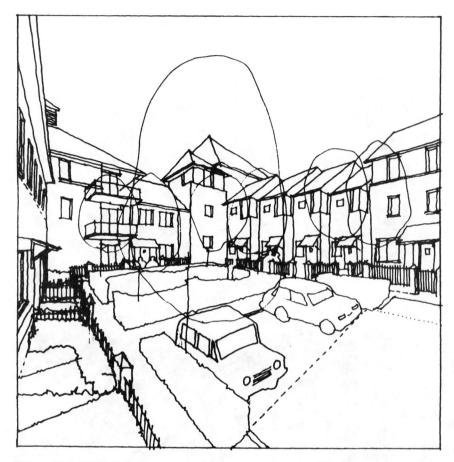

Figure 11.5 *(b) Sketch view*

Promoter's reponse

Brent Council accepted the jury's decision which was quickly ratified by the relevant committee (the Housing and General Purposes Sub-Committee) following a detailed presentation by the winning team.

Outcome

Council officers and the winning team prepared an outline SRB submission in May 1994 with a full formal submission in September 1994. SRB funding for the first phase was achieved in December 1994.

Case study 6   Langdon Cliffs Visitor Facilities, Dover 1993

Introduction

Type of competition
A selection procedure based on the architectural competition format.

Subject
Improved information and facilities for visitors and accommodation for wardens at Langdon Cliffs, Dover, Kent.

Project value
The budget for the proposed building works and immediate landscaping was set at £600 000.

Promoter
The competition was promoted and organised by the Kent and East Sussex Regional Office of the National Trust.

Manager
The competition was managed by Pierce Hill Associates, a Kent-based firm specialising in development consultancy and project management. Their duties included organising the whole selection procedure, drawing up the brief and advising on costs.

Assessors
The judging panel was selected by the National Trust (NT). All its members had some links with the Trust – three were officers and the other three were members of its Architectural Panel (AP).
   The judges were:

Rodney Melville, RIBA: Chairperson (AP member)
Selina Ballance, RIBA: AP chairperson
Dan Cruikshank, Hon FRIBA: Architectural journalist and writer (AP member)
Sir Angus Stirling: Director General of the National Trust
John Chesshyre: NT Regional Historic Buildings Representative
Peter Battrick: NT Regional Public Affairs Manager

Key points

The National Trust's policy is to commission architects who are recognised for good quality contemporary work. The Langdon Cliffs site was considered to be a particularly challenging one in view of its physical prominence at the nationally symbolic White Cliffs of Dover. It is also designated AONB (Area of Outstanding

Natural Beauty), is part of the Heritage Coast and lies within an SSSI (Site of Specific Scientific Interest). Any building had to meet stringent planning requirements, satisfy a range of interest groups and counter criticism against further development of the site.

It was against this background that the Trust decided to promote a competition 'to secure a building which would embody best current practice in relation to environmental concerns'. Aware of current criticisms of competitions and advised by its standing Architectural Advisory Panel, the Trust took great care in drawing up a procedure which, it hoped, would be acceptable to all those with an interest in the project and to the architects invited to take part. This approach paid dividends. While the competition did not entirely succeed in avoiding dispute, the openness of the briefing and the opportunities it gave for discussion did help to ease the consultative processes. Detailed planning consent was given by Dover District Council about six months after the selection of the architect.

Approach

The Trust sought the advice of Pierce Hill Associates, who were subsequently appointed as managers, as to appropriate methods of developing the site. Taking into account the high profile of the client and the sensitive nature of the site, Pierce Hill recommended the Trust to consider an architectural competition. It set out to follow the RIBA guidelines but considered RIBA endorsement 'an unnecessary additional expense'. In the event, the guidelines were adapted to give the Trust more control over the selection of the winner (i.e. interviews were built into the selection process and the judging panel comprised NT officers and panel members). A careful pre-selection was carried out:

> The client should be confident that they will be able to work with the selected architect. Personalities are an equally important consideration as qualifications. The objective of the selection process is to arrive at a team that will provide the client with the building they want on time and on budget.

The delicacy of the planning negotiations led the promoters to put a special clause into the conditions to ensure that they were able to keep control of the post-competition debate. The payments to the participants were made subject to the following condition:

> Participants agree not to release any details of their submissions for publication until planning permission is secured for the winning entry or until such time as the National Trust give permission.

(The Trust stated its intention to mount an exhibition of all the schemes once planning permission had been obtained. Each of the unsuccessful participants was offered a payment of £1500.)

Competitors were assured of the Trust's 'good intent' by the inclusion in the conditions of the following statement:

> In the unlikely event of the project not proceeding to an architectural appointment the winning entry will receive an enhanced award of £10 000 in lieu of appointment.

Competition format

The Trust used the expertise available within its own organisation to draw up a 'longlist' of 42 practices. Each one was contacted and invited to register interest and send in brochures of its work. The invitation made clear that declining to enter would not count against the practice: 'If on this occasion you are not in a position to register an interest in this competition it should be emphasised that this will not influence future consideration of your practice for similar competitions.' Only two practices declined through pressure of other work (both part of the 'international competition circuit'). On the basis of the information submitted, 20 out of the remaining 40 firms were sent a preliminary brief and asked to respond by setting out their initial approach. No money was offered at this stage. The Trust sought to limit the amount of work done by the architects by requiring only a written report of 500 words, though many architects added sketches to illustrate their ideas.

The judging panel then selected 12 practices which they visited at their own offices. (This cut down on the amount of time the architects had to spend on travelling and gave the judges a further opportunity to assess the way they worked.) Seven practices were shortlisted to take part in the next stage. These were, in the main, smaller scale London-based practices which had been successful in other competitions. One local practice was included. The seven competitors were:

Le Fevre Wood and Royle, Rye, Sussex
Pawson Williams, London
Penoyre and Prasad, London
Peter Inskip and Peter Jenkins, London
Stanton Williams, London
Tim Ronalds, London
van Heyningen and Haward, London.

A more detailed briefing document was circulated and competitors were given two weeks in which to study the brief and send written questions to the competition manager. This was followed by a forum – an open discussion meeting between representatives of all seven practices and the panel of judges. The forum enabled individual practices to question and clarify the brief while ensuring that every competitor had access to the same information.

The competitors were given a further six weeks in which to develop their designs. They were required to submit no more than six A1 sheets supported by a brief written report. It was suggested that the presentations should equate to 'sketch' design (comparable to RIBA Workstage C). Models and 'glossy' presentations were specifically excluded.

An innovation on the standard procedure was that the services of the quantity surveyors appointed as advisers to the Trust were made available to each of the competitors. The aim was to ensure that all seven schemes met the financial criteria and were working to a common standard. This QS advice enabled competitors to amend their designs, where necessary, before they submitted them for assessment. (It is common practice for one firm of quantity surveyors to work with several competitors in a major competition and architects accept that no cross referencing takes place.) The procedure used by the Trust meant that each scheme was working to the same cost analysis basis, thus avoiding differences of opinion between the promoter's cost consultants and the consultants of the different competitors.

The final designs were examined by a team of advisers comprising specialist NT staff, planning consultants, quantity surveyors and representatives from the Dover Society and the NT Regional Committee. They worked to checklists prepared by the manager. This information was given to the judging panel when it met to assess the submissions.

Competitors were asked to be available during the judging. The intention was that the panel could seek clarification of any points which worried them. In the event, three of the seven were interviewed. This was regarded as providing the Trust with an additional safeguard. Asked whether the winning team would have been selected had the schemes been judged anonymously in the second stage, the Manager confirmed that 'it answered all the requirements of the brief and had stood out right from the technical assessment stage'.

Brief

The brief was written by Pierce Hill drawing on work done by John Chesshyre, the Trust's Historic Buildings representative for the Kent and East Sussex Region. The planning section was prepared by consultants following detailed discussion with the relevant authorities and interested parties.

The brief set out the requirements for the building in terms of siting, design, traffic and parking, landscaping, nature conservation, planning and finance. It also detailed the spaces and facilities to be provided and gave guidance on materials and maintenance. The main (second stage) brief was a concise document covering no more than fifteen sides of A4, including the competition conditions. More detailed information on specific aspects (e.g. history of the site, location of underground chambers, etc.) was given in appendices as was information on site levels and services. Competitors were also provided with a site plan and location map. Relevant legislative requirements were identified and referenced within the brief.

The criteria for assessment were set out and clear distinctions made between mandatory requirements and desirable objectives. The brief also told competitors what was not required and what would be regarded as unacceptable. For example, under 'Siting', the brief stated 'The National Trust will not entertain a submission that sites the proposed facilities to the south of the skidding sheds ... should any competitor view this as an unacceptable condition they must declare so to the Manager as soon as possible'.

Costs and prizes

In terms of actual expenditure the cost of the selection procedure was not high. The six unsuccessful competitors were each paid £1500 (Stage C fees for a project of this size would work out at between two and three times this amount). The full management service was undertaken for a fee of £7000. Documentation was kept to a simple production format. The main cost to the Trust was that of staff and consultancy time, both in preparing the brief and in selecting the architect. The initial selection process was a protracted one – involving meetings, visits and interviews. These costs have been estimated at £50 000.

Timetable

Initial invitation	2 September 1993
Outline brief circulated to selected competitors	27 September 1993
First-stage submission by	22 October 1993
Second-stage brief circulated	22 November 1993
Questions by	29 November 1993
Forum	7 December 1993
Second-stage submissions	14 January 1994
Judging panel meeting	21 January 1994

The result was made public in October 1994 (after planning permission had been obtained).

Winner's approach

The Trust appointed van Heyningen and Haward as architects for the project. Their response to the brief was a long, low building which they saw as a centrepiece for a potential rolling programme of improvements to the whole site. Its keynotes were flexibility, simplicity and design quality. The architects expressed a great enthusiasm for the place which they anticipated would be shared by those who visited. The proposed building took care to provide undercover space 'which is neither truly internal nor external' so that outdoor activities could be pursued whatever the weather. The structure was one of a grid of columns supporting the wooden beams of a low pitch roof. The columns were brick clad and the timber purlins were left exposed giving a warm, open interior which would be relatively low cost and easy to maintain. Brick and wood were also used on the exterior of the building with its impact on the surrounding area being further reduced by a grass roof.

The architects envisaged that the whole centre could be built within a twenty-eight week contract period.

Promoter's response

The Trust believes that the winning scheme justified the amount of effort which it put into the competition and that the result fulfils its policy of creating a heritage for the future.

Outcome

The winning scheme received planning consent in September 1994. Work was scheduled to start on site immediately.

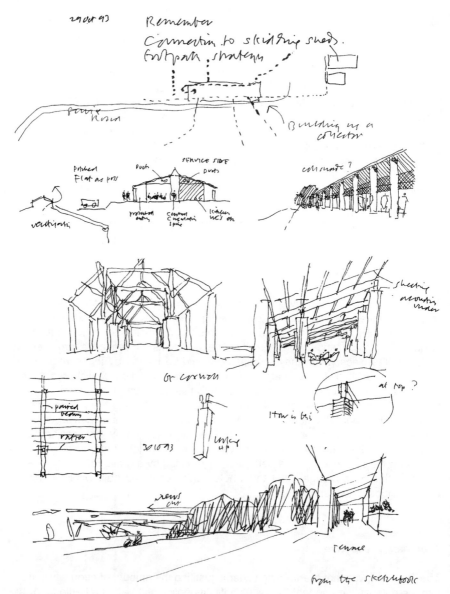

Figure 11.6 *(a) Sketches from the competition report. Architects: van Heyningen and Haward*

Figure 11.6 *(b) The meeting area; (c) Inside–outside space, the covered entrance*

Case study 7   South Downs Health NHS Trust competitions: Moulsecoomb Clinic and Newhaven Downs Hospital, Sussex 1993 and 1994

This case study looks at two separate competitions. They are linked together here because they were promoted consecutively as part of a defined procurement policy, drawn up by the promoter with the intent of bringing new ideas and approaches into the design of health care facilities. The chairman of the South Downs Health NHS Trust, architect John Wells-Thorpe, developed the policy and co-ordinated the competition procedures. Although his professional experience was beneficial in that it helped him state the case for introducing the competition system into the commissioning of the health care buildings, the procedures followed did not rely on his professional expertise for their success.

The competition system was initially used to secure a design approach for a small health centre building. This was intended to test out procedures and to demonstrate to the client organisation that the system would work effectively. Its success, in terms of both the procedures used and the quality of design achieved, led directly to the second competition being held for a larger project. Continuity between the two competitions was made a specific objective. Sir Philip Powell was appointed as the Senior Architect Assessor in both competitions, with the winnning architect from the first competition being invited to act as one of the assessors on the next. A consistent approach was followed and the South Downs Health NHS Trust managers who had been involved in the first competition met with their colleagues who were to organise and assess the second in order to pass on the experience they had gained.

Both competitions were managed by the RIBA Competitions Office working in close association with the promoting organisation, the South Downs Health NHS Trust.

This case study sets out the details of each individual competition and then goes on to look at the overall approach and assess its success.

Moulsecoomb Clinic, 1993

Introduction

Type of competition
A single stage competition limited to six invited practices. The promoter choice option was used (two winning schemes).

Subject
The competition was for the design of a small clinic on the Moulsecoomb Estate, on the outskirts of Brighton, Sussex to replace facilities housed in a portacabin building.

Project value
Moulsecoomb Clinic was valued at £600 000 (1994 prices).

Assessors
Sir Philip Powell: Senior Architect Assessor
Alan Deacon: Second Architect Assessor
Jan Anson: Area Director, Community Health Services in Brighton (SDH)
Lynn Dodd: Team Manager for staff based at the clinic (SDH)

Key points

Although the first competition promoted by the South Downs Health NHS Trust was limited to six invited practices, it was seen as providing an opportunity to extend the normal commissioning procedure.

Six widely differing practices were selected: some private, some public, some local, some regional in scope. Equally important, some practices were included which had no experience of the design of health buildings. They were selected on the basis of the quality of their work in other areas in the hope that they would bring with them new insights and interpretations.

The Trust also used the competition process to draw in both staff and public. A small technical panel was set up comprising community nurses, health visiters, GPs and local councillors who were consulted and kept informed throughout the process.

Approach

In the introduction to the brief for the Moulsecoomb Clinic, the promoter writes:

> The whole purpose of running an architectural competition is to elicit new ideas that go beyond stylistic reinterpretations. It is important that each competitor gets the real 'feel' for the area, and the resulting design must be both welcoming and buoyant in feeling but at the same time reflect the need for security. The same is true of the interior in that it needs to be warm and reassuring so that the continuing breakdown of artificial barriers between 'them and us' can be maintained.

Competition format

Six practices were selected by South Downs Health (SDH) with the approval of the RIBA. The brief was circulated and, after a period for study, a question and answer session was held. Instead of the 'colloquium' format, each practice was invited individually and sequentially. This provided the opportunity for competitors to clarify the promoter's requirements and explore possible approaches without having to share their ideas with others. The meetings were between the competitors and the assessors but local health care managers were also present to answer questions on their particular areas of concern.

The six competitors then developed their designs and submitted them on an anonymous basis. The material submitted was to follow a simple format:

- 1:100 scale plans;
- 1:100 elevations and two section;

- site plan and location plan:
- a perspective sketch of the exterior and/or interior from a natural viewpoint.

These were to be contained on no more than three A1 sheets and accompanied by a report of not more than two A4 sides giving an explanation of the competitor's proposal, including clear reference to choice of materials.

The six schemes were studied by the technical and user panels who transmitted their views to the assessors. The designs were also displayed at the old clinic so that those with an interest could comment. The assessors selected two schemes both of which were considered to be capable of being developed and reported their decision to the promoter. The two winning practices were invited to present their schemes to the promoter so that the final decision could be made. One of these two schemes was designed by an architect experienced in health care buildings while the other was by an architect entering a new area of work. The promoter appointed the latter.

While a detailed brief was issued to competitors, the promoter stressed that the competition was for a sketch design. The aim was to identify an approach which could be developed though a detailed dialogue between the client and the appointed architect. The competition was seen as providing a valuable learning experience for the health care staff which enabled them to participate more effectively in the dialogue at design development stage.

Brief

The objective of the competition was to seek new ideas which challenge current thought about designing for community health care.

A detailed brief was issued to competitors to give them an overview of the requirements. The competition, however, concentrated on the design approach and the criteria for this were established in the introduction to the briefing document (see 'Approach' above). The brief looked at the community the building was designed to serve, the philosophy of health care provision in the area and the uses to be accommodated. The emphasis throughout the brief was on identifying what the building was to be for – who was to use it and what they would do – rather than specifying details of space and provision.

The briefing process was seen as starting before the competition was launched and continuing once the architect had been appointed. The question and answer meetings were regarded as part of the process.

Timetable

The competition was held during the first half of 1993 on a similar timetable to that set out for the Newhaven Downs Hospital (see below).

Costs and prizes

An honorarium of £1500 was paid to each of the six practices with the winner being appointed as architect for the project.

Winner's approach

The winning scheme, designed by the Sussex practice, Michael Blee Design, responds to the challenges set in the brief by offering a warm and welcoming building, carefully designed to disguise the concern for security.

The accommodation is provided around two interior courtyards: one providing the core of the main area of activity; the other offering quiet retreat.

The architect describes his approach:

> My focus was on the nature of the hill-side site and the achievement of a perceptible image of the relationship between the multiplicity of rooms and functions as soon as the clinic was entered. It was of prime importance that visitors should have an immediate sense of the geography of the building and not get 'lost'. This and an (immediate) awareness of structure and form bathed in light. Clearly my Church work, my predeliction for natural materials and particularly timber, my delight in structure and construction of light cloisters around courtyards, were all present during the early stages.

Outcome

The clinic was opened in January 1994 and is well-liked by all its users, both health staff and public.

Newhaven Downs Hospital, 1994

Introduction

Type of competition
The Newhaven Downs Hospital competition (1994) was organised on the same basis as the previous competition. As the project was larger, it had first to be advertised in the *EC Journal*. Seven competitors were selected from this wider entry base.

Subject
A nursing home and day-care facilities and polyclinic at Newhaven, Sussex to replace outdated, nineteenth-century accommodation.

Project value
The maximum funding to meet building and engineering costs is £2 350 000 based upon NHS departmental cost allowances.

Assessors
Sir Philip Powell: Senior Architect Assessor
Dr Michael Blee: Second Architect Assessor (winner of the first competition)
Michael Donkin: Project sponsor (SDH)
Andrew Hughes: Project manager (SDH)

Approach

Competitors were selected from a range of design backgrounds and with different design philosophies so as to provide a wide variety of approaches.

Once again the aim was to bring new ideas to bear on health care provision. The chairman of the Trust writes:

> For far too long, the care of the elderly and mentally infirm has been regarded as insufficiently 'glamorous' or intellectually engaging to attract many of the high fliers in the NHS, and for related reasons has also found itself categorised as a lower priority than was justified when it came to new buildings. . . . The aim of this competition is not only to design a group of lighter, brighter buildings but to try and break entirely new ground in reinterpreting the needs of occupants and staff alike, and discovering ways in which good architecture can not only meet the demanding needs of the new health care philosophy, but can further suggest, by its configuration and treatment, new horizons which will encourage staff to see new possibilities and so stimulate the duller senses of the elderly without confusing them. A tough task – but that is why we are holding a competition.

Competition format

The same procedures were followed as in the first competition and the same specification was given to competitors regarding the material to be submitted.

Brief

The principles established in the first competition were used in the second. The competitors were given a detailed brief with a package of supporting information to set the context but were asked to address the key criteria at the competition stage. The brief was 'designed to provide an insight into the philosophy and style of care that the Trust wishes to promote and to give some detail of the services to be provided from the site'. In developing their solutions, the architects were asked to provide schemes which were 'innovative, welcoming, workable and respond well to the environment in which they must operate'.

Timetable

Competition launched	December 1993
Questions and answers	13 January 1994
Submission of designs	8 March 1994
Assessment of designs	22 March 1994
Appointment of design team	early April 1994
Planning approval	July 1994
Start on site	January 1995

Figure 11.7 *(a) Moulescoomb Clinic. Architect: Michael Blee Design. Photograph: David Hatfull*

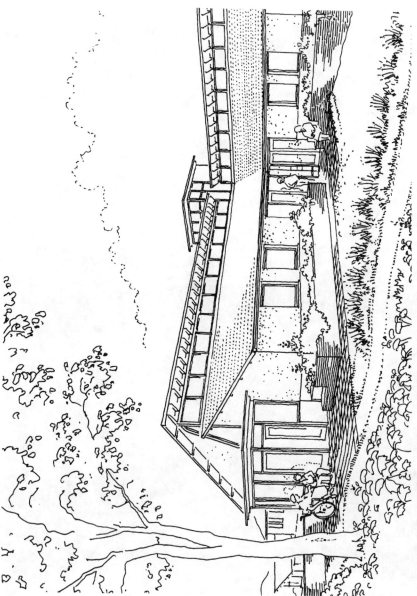

Figure 11.7 *(b) Newhaven Downs Hospital. Architects: Penoyre and Prasad*

Winner's approach

The winning design, submitted by the London-based practice of Penoyre and Prasad, proposed a series of domestic scale buildings with views over the pleasant wooded surroundings. They outline their aims as follows:

> The design aims to put the needs of the patient first. The building will accommodate long-stay, short-stay and respite care. There will be a particularly diverse set of clients – from frail elderly people with limited mobility to people with dementia who may be profoundly confused. The building will provide a comforting and comfortable environment which will also be stimulating to the senses.

Promoter's reponse

The promoter was pleased with the results of the dual competition exerise both in terms of the quality of buildings it had produced and in terms of increased staff awareness of the value of good design and commitment to the projects.

Further commissions were made in 1995, building on the experience gained in the two competitions. Though they took the 'short cut route' of interviewing selected practices without asking for design work, much of what had been learnt in the two competitions was fed back into these selection processes. Architects who had produced interesting proposals in the two competitions were interviewed for these other projects.

Case study 8   New College for Durham University at Howlands Farm, Durham 1994

Introduction

Type of competition
A two-stage competition with a pre-selection process for entry to the first stage. One single winner selected by the jury of assessors.

This was the first competition to be organised by the RIBA as a design contest in accordance with the EC Services Directive which came into force in January 1994. Care was taken to follow the directive to the letter and the promoter sought legal advice as to how the requirement to maintain anonymity throughout the process should be interpreted. The competition was open to UK architects and architects registered under the EC Architects' Directive (EC Directive 85-384).

Subject
The design of a new college providing residential accommodation for 600 students and up to 35 members of staff, on an open site (known as Howlands Farm) on the southern edge of Durham city.

Project value
The initial development costs were estimated to be £15–£20 m.

Promoter
The University of Durham.

Manager
The RIBA Competitions Office.

Assessors
The judging panel comprised two architects nominated by the RIBA and two nominees of the promoter. They were:

Professor Evelyn Ebsworth: Vice-Chancellor, University of Durham
Miss Deborah Lavin: President, Howlands Trust
John Partridge CBE: RIBA Senior Architect Assessor
Tom Kay: RIBA Second Assessor

Key points

The quality of the site, hill-top farmland forming part of a strategically important green space surrounding the central urban area of Durham, required special criteria to be met. Its development constituted 'a major departure from the Local Plan' (Director of

Technical Services, Durham City Council) and sensitive handling was crucial if full planning consent was to be gained (see 'Brief' below).

In order to promote the new college, the University established the Howlands Trust. At an early stage in its programme, the Trust arranged three Artists' Forums at which a group of artists, design professionals and ecologists were invited to consider the design criteria for creating an academic community on this site. A number of the criteria which emerged were incorporated into the briefing process (see 'Artists' forums' below). The Trust also organised a competition for school children.

Background

Durham University, which is organised on the collegiate system, doubled in size during the period 1973–93, accommodating the growth in extensions to the existing colleges. In order to meet the needs of students and the local community into the next century and recognising that the existing colleges had reached the limit of their capacity to extend further, the University planned an additional new college.

Approach

As a publicly funded body, the University was required to use one of the EC procedures to select design consultants for a project of this size. Given what has been described as a 'stunning' site in a high profile situation and the need to attract funding for the project, the University was aware that it had to secure 'a quality imaginative design'. It decided to promote a competition and was encouraged to do so by the Planning Department of Durham City Council as well as by both English Heritage and the Royal Fine Art Commission. The University already had experience of organising a competition and was aware of the amount of work it involved so appointed the RIBA to manage the whole process (a service which had not been available previously). John Partridge, senior partner of the London-based architectural practice HKPA, was nominated as the Senior Assessor and appointed at an early stage in the process. The arrangements for the competition were drawn up by the University in consultation with the Competition Manager and the Senior Assessor.

Because of the size and scope of the project, the University invited entries from 'architect-led design teams embracing the full range of professional skills required for the design and supervision of a contract to construct the development'. It was also decided to 'pre-select' the first-stage competitors rather than have a fully open competition. This decision was made on the advice of the RIBA to cut down on the amount of abortive work. It also provided some safeguards to the promoter who was able to select the teams best suited to a project of this scale. This selection procedure was clearly explained in the announcement placed in the *EC Journal*. At this stage the University invited people to register their interest, but stated: 'Registration for the competition does not necessarily guarantee participation in it.' Those registered were sent a preliminary information pack setting out the competition conditions and outlining the basic design requirements. This initial briefing document gave background information about the University and the city of Durham, the need for the new college, a summary of strategic design objectives and an indication of costs. A small scale contoured site plan and a context plan were included. Those wishing to take part in the competition were asked to submit evidence that they had experience of similar work and/or work which they considered demonstrated a capability appropriate to the project. Practice information including details of the staff who would be responsible for the design and implementation of the project was also required. A non-returnable registration fee of £30 was charged.

Initially the University intended that the assessors should select the teams to be invited to take part in the first stage of the competition. Following legal advice, it was determined that this would contravene the EC requirement on anonymity. The University then set up a small in-house team, advised by an architect nominated by the RIBA, to select the competitors.

Competition format

There were 157 registered applications. (Fewer than ten were from outside the UK though several others were teams comprising European and UK firms.) The applications were shortlisted to 21, including some local practices and two from outside the UK. Each selected competitor was sent a copy of the brief and allowed one week in which to submit written questions only. They were also told of the arrangements for visiting the site. A 'statement of response to questions' was circulated and competitors were given a further three weeks to prepare outline designs. No further contact between the competitors and the promoting body was permitted. At the end of this stage competitors were required to submit 'no more than three A2 landscape sheets and a maximum of four A4 sheets to supplement the A2 panels'. Competitors were allowed to use these 'to demonstrate their ideas graphically and/or in writing'. The submission was to address the following:

- the perception and understanding of the college and its anatomy;
- creative response to the brief;
- diagram of intent for the use of the site especially in relation to:
  a)   the hill
  b)   the road
  c)   the access
  d)   the boundaries
  e)   the views
  f)   the need for shelter on an exposed site
  g)   the city of Durham;
- character and design philosophy of the proposed development.

The aim was to direct attention at this stage towards concepts and relationships. Six schemes were selected by the assessors each of which demonstrated a different way of approaching the development of the site. The selected teams were:

Arup Associates,
Downs and Variava,
Greenfield Jones Partnership,
Percy Thomas Partnership,
Shepheard Epstein Hunter,
Studio Granada.

The brief was slightly amended for the second stage. Competitors were required to submit eight × A1 sheets showing:

- a site plan at 1:1000 and at least one section at 1:1000;
- full plans and sections of all buildings at 1:200;
- elevations of all buildings at 1:100 sufficient to describe the appearance of the whole scheme;
- plan, section and elevation through a selected part of the building plan at 1:50 of all sets/room groupings with suggested room layouts;
- three-dimensional drawings to illustrate the design and/or photographs of models (models themselves were not accepted).

Prior to the competition, the University commissioned a Passive Engineering study (by R W Gregory and Partners): this produced a computer model against which various aspects of the energy efficiency of submitted schemes could be assessed. A team of technical advisers went through each scheme making a detailed analysis of costs, structure, engineering and landscaping and prepared a report for the assessors. The University initially had a problem with appointing technical advisers as many of those approached were planning to work with competitors. For this reason, competitors were asked to complete a pro-forma and send it to the RIBA Competitions Office with their entry. The pro-formas were detached on receipt. This enabled the promoters to identify which consultants would be free to act as technical advisers.

The competition conditions gave the assessors the opportunity to select three equal winners but, in the event, the University decided it wanted the awards to be ranked. The scheme eventually placed first emerged as a clear winner early in the process but long deliberations were held as to the practicality of certain innovative design solutions (e.g. windtowers were used to circulate warm air through the buildings and also to provide 'free' ventilation). The assessors satisfied themselves that such proposals had been well-researched and that, should they present problems, alternatives could be found without detracting from the overall quality of the approach.

The assessors awarded first and second prizes (to Arup Associates and Shepheard Epstein Hunter respectively) and honoraria were given to the remaining second-stage competitors. The winning team was appointed by the promoter on a negotiated fee, the basis of which was set out in the conditions.

Artists' forums

The three forums were held to stimulate thinking from the outset by asking a group of people 'for whom the aesthetic was a natural first principle' to explore the theoretical possibilities of the site and the community. A continuing association with the project was established. The principles proposed 'to inform rather than proscribe' were as follows:

- Variety: of uses, spaces, sizes and form.
- Economy: land is precious: use the minimum area, saving the rest for an uncertain future. Use the spaces between the buildings.

- Conservation: retain the site's present basic form; remove nothing from it; re-use spoil, sculpt the site; include textures derived from the site itself.
- Integration: with surrounding land use; soften edges and contextualize the scheme; increase woodland edge and wetland habitat, plan new hedges and trees to be part of the architectural design.
- Seclusion: minimise pollution from road noise and intrusion by vehicles onto the site.

Brief

The brief was a clear and concise document which established the parameters for development while keeping mandatory requirements to the minimum. It was drawn up by Richard Metcalfe, Director of the Estates and Buildings Department of the University of Durham.

The core of the brief was the schedule of accommodation. This detailed requirements in terms of number and size (minimum total floor area) of the study bedrooms, support facilities, staff accommodation and communal spaces. It was supported by a separate section setting out the design criteria. These included such considerations as value for money, energy efficiency, environmental policy, disabled access, and safety and security. Flexibility was seen as important to enable both phasing and expansion.

No detailed planning brief was given but a statement prepared by the Director of Technical Services of Durham City Council was included 'for supplementary guidance'. This set out the context in which the outline planning permission was given and made reference to the relevant documentation. There was also a section on site conditions based on a geotechnical report prepared by Exploration Associates.

The briefing documents were introduced by 'a personal statement from the President of the Howlands Trust' (Deborah Lavin, also one of the assessors) in which she looked at the principles which lay behind the new development. Ideas of what constitutes a college community (a scholastic village?) were explored. 'Variety', 'individualism', 'interaction' were identified as key words for both the function and the design. Concepts of what constitutes public and private space were developed (places to gather for conversation and celebration, places to study and relax without isolation). This set the context for an assessment to be made of each scheme in terms of its potential contribution to the ethos of the new college.

Costs

The costs directly related to the competition came to £7750 (including the RIBA's fee and the fees of the two assessors). Other costs, including staff time, general expenses, etc. were more difficult to quantify as some of the work would have to have been done in any commissioning process.

Prizes totalling £25 000 were awarded to the two prize winners (the first prize as an advance on the professional fee), with honoraria of £5000 paid to each of the remaining second stage participants.

Timetable

Notice faxed to *EC Journal* office	31 January 1994
Announcement in *EC Journal*	11 February 1994
Closing date for registration	9 March 1994
Issue of first stage brief	19 April 1994
Deadline for questions	25 April 1994
Statement of answers issued	4 May 1994
Submission of first-stage material	24 May 1994
First-stage assessment	26–27 May 1994
Invitation to second-stage competitors	1 June 1994
Deadline for questions	10 June 1994
Answers to questions	20 June 1994
Submission of second-stage material	10 August 1994
Second-stage assessment	15–16 August 1994
Architects appointed	6 December 1994

Winner's approach

The winning team outlined its approach in the introductory paragraphs of the competition report:

It is significant that the brief implies a collaboration between the University and their chosen designers. They aim to be involved.

Our submission is about ideas, not finite solutions. The concept shows a setting of sufficient strength to contain the college in a relaxed and small scale architecture which is easily built, maintained and adapted.

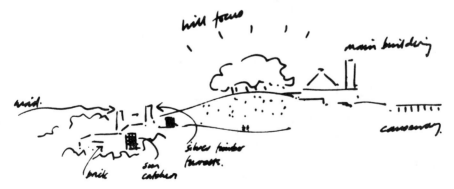

Figure 11.8a

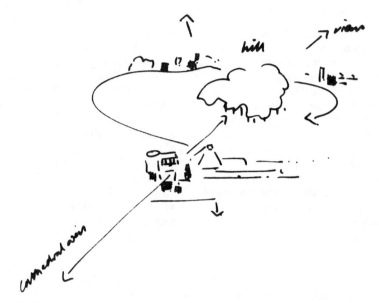

Figure 11.8b

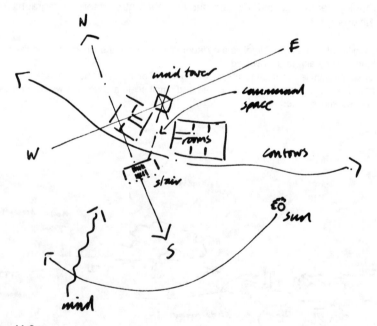

Figure 11.8c

'Adapted' here means not only change during the existence of the college but during its creation. In other words there is room for design colloboration. Therefore the design details asked for in the brief are ordered by 3 overriding propositions:

- A stunning, permanent, sheltering and secure landscape
- Climate as energy source expressed in architecture
- Materials and methods of construction consistent with an English landscape setting.

(The illustrations in this text are taken from the competition report.)

Promoter's response

The University was delighted with the outcome of the competition in producing a design of such high quality which produced an excellent starting point for dialogue in developing a detailed design.

Outcome

In December 1994, Arup Associates were appointed by the University to progress the scheme to planning application stage, and the University commenced a detailed assessment of the costs in relation to securing funding for the project.

Case study 9   South Bank Centre, London 1994

Introduction

Type of competition
A selection procedure for a Master Planner.

Subject
The regeneration of the South Bank Arts Centre; taking into consideration its existing buildings, its immediate surroundings and its relationships with adjacent areas on both sides of the River Thames.

Project value
The estimated value of the project (core site work only) is £60 million.

Promoter
The South Bank Board.

Manager
The competition was run by the South Bank Centre with Gordon Graham, Past President of the RIBA, acting as adviser throughout the process. Architects, DEGW (London) were appointed to produce the brief.

Assessors
The panel of eight assessors was chaired by Sir Brian Corby, Chairman of the South Bank Board. The other members were:

Eldred Evans: Architect (UK)
Anish Kapoor: Artist and sculptor
Henry Meyric Hughes: Director of Exhibitions (South Bank Centre)
Christian de Portzamparc: Architect (France)
Martin Smith: South Bank Board member
Nicholas Snowman: Chief Executive (South Bank Centre)
Alan Stanton: Architect (UK)

Key points

The Centre comprises an internationally known set of arts buildings on one of the most significant sites in the country (both geographically and politically). The buildings include the Royal Festival Hall (listed Grade 1), the Hayward Gallery and the Queen Elizabeth Hall. The area, which runs along the south bank of the Thames, is also home to the Museum of the Moving Image and the National Theatre (these are under separate ownership). It is dissected by both rail and road bridges which cause problems with access and circulation. The successful designer not only has to reconcile a multiplicity of interests but to do so in the context of a high profile and historically controversial situation.

Background

The South Bank Centre evolved from the 1951 Festival of Britain when the original site was cleared and the Royal Festival Hall built. The arts facilities were built and, for the most part, run first by the London County Council and then by its successor, the Greater London Council. When the Greater London Council was abolished by the government, the buildings and the land they occupied passed to the Arts Council of Great Britain which leased them to the South Bank Board, a trust specially constituted for this purpose. The Board inherited a powerful but physically run-down collection of arts resources in an area fraught with problems. While the Centre received substantial revenue grants from the Arts Council, the Board had very limited access to capital funds. Links were established with a developer and various proposals drawn up. The aim was to develop the site commercially in order to finance the improvement of the arts buildings. In 1991 the Board released a master plan which proposed the demolition of the 1960s buildings and their replacement with office buildings. New arts facilities were included on another part of the site. The scheme served to focus opposition to the commercial development of the site, adding impetus to the debate about the future of the whole area. It also led to a reappraisal being made of the 1960s buildings. The recession finally buried the commercially-based option and with it the developer link. The advent of the lottery offered a possible source of funds for a major regeneration scheme, this time based on the retention of the existing buildings and the predominantly arts-related use of the site.

Approach

The South Bank Board sought the advice of the Architecture Foundation (see page 42) which recommended a design competition. Gordon Graham was appointed as co-ordinator. Because of the complexity of the project, in terms of both design and implementation, it was decided to search for an architect to masterplan the development rather than for a detailed design scheme for the site and its buildings. The Board wanted somebody with whom they could work over a period of several years to develop the Centre as the core of an arts quarter and as an integral part of the whole area. They were strongly advised to follow the 'designer selection method' which provided for interviews at each stage in the assessment.

Competition format

The format followed one of open invitation; pre-selection (10 teams); and a staged submission process.

The competition was advertised and architects and urbanists were invited to 'express interest in the selection procedure for the appointment of a master planner for the regeneration of the South Bank site'. No documentation was circulated at this stage. The basic details were set out in the advertisements, asking those interested to submit:

- Full particulars of the individual, firm or design team;
- Information on relevant previous work, experience or interests;

- References to the publication of previous work or projects. No more than three sheets of photographs or other images were to be submitted;
- Two sides of A4 text to provide a brief statement about the role of cultural centres in the 21st century, either with reference to the South Bank Centre, or in general terms.

One hundred and twenty-one submissions were received from which a shortlist of ten was made. The selected participants were:

Allies and Morrison, London
Jeremy Dixon and Edward Jones, London
Sir Norman Foster and Partners, London
Gregotti Associates International, Milan
Michael Hopkins and Partners, London
Lifschutz Davidson, London
MacCormac Jamieson Pritchard, London
Martorell Bohigas Mackay and Puigdomenech, Barcelona
Richard Rogers Partnership, London
Troughton McAslan, London

Each practice was given a copy of the brief and, after a one month period for study, was invited to send representatives to a two-day collective briefing session at the South Bank Centre. The competitors then had two further months in which to prepare the initial design approach. At the end of this period, each team was asked to present its proposals to the jury of assessors.

For this stage competitors were asked to submit:

- an illustrated report in A3 landscape format;
- not more than three A0 sheets mounted on lightweight board to reproduce illustrations and diagrams to summarise the key features of the submission;
- photographs of sketch models were permitted, but no actual models were to be accepted.

The report was to address both the core site and the wider area. The architects were not asked to consider the design of individual buildings (existing or proposed).

Three finalists were selected: Allies and Morrison, Michael Hopkins and Partners, Richard Rogers Partnership. They were briefed individually and given time to develop, substantiate or clarify particular aspects of their proposals. For example, one team was asked to demonstrate the technical feasibility of the glazed structure which it proposed should cover the Queen Elizabeth Hall and Hayward Gallery. A final round of presentations was arranged and the winner selected.

Note: The term 'competition' was never used by the promoters who always referred to the 'selection procedure'. This term may have been used to establish the distinction between this method and that of the EC 'design contest' which requires anonymity to be observed throughout the process.

Consultation and public involvement

By reason of its ownership, position and history, the whole of the South Bank area had become a focus for the political battles of the 1980s, generating a climate of distrust. At the same time, it was evident that the different interests could only be served by some form of co-operative initiative. The regeneration of the Arts Centre was integrally linked to that of the surrounding area. Consultation was seen as crucial to the success of the project.

Public exhibitions were held at the Architecture Foundation and the Royal Festival Hall to launch the competition and visitors were asked for their views. A discussion forum was held (organised by Academy Editions which subsequently published a book on the competition) to which various groups with an interest in the project were invited. Meetings were held with a range of organisations to establish the context in which the Centre would operate. These included funding bodies and arts organisations; owners of adjacent buildings and sites and their consultants (several adjacent developments were being planned); and the planning, river and transport authorities.

When the result was announced, an exhibition was mounted showing all the second-stage designs, including detailed models. Once again, visiters were invited to give their views. About forty separate presentations (breakfast, lunch and evening sessions) were made to specially invited groups. All those who had taken part in the pre-briefing consultations were invited back as well as local amenity groups, environmental organisations, tourist interests, MPs and councillors.

Brief

DEGW had a team of people working on the brief. They identified the competition as 'an opportunity for the rebirth of the South Bank' dividing the areas to be addressed into 'the core site' and 'the wider area'. Three 'headline' requirements were established: accessibility; creative partnership; place.

The objective of the competition was stated in the briefing document:

> The South Bank Centre now requires a directing and unifying concept. The purpose of this selection procedure is to discover a master planner who has the imagination to transform an arid environment and a bundle of heterogeneous buildings into a clearly defined, easily perceptible arts centre which emphasises the strengths of individual art forms at the same time as making possible and encouraging fluid communication between them.

The brief was directed towards giving competitors sufficient information to achieve that objective. Its function was seen as one of establishing the contraints and opportunities, clarifying and prioritising demand and agreeing a framework and timetable in which the architect could work. A number of 'perceived problems' were identified. It was left to competitors to suggest solutions.

DEGW sought to provide information on the existing buildings (some listed, others considered to be worthy of listing), the political background (the people's place?), patterns of use (changes in the way the arts are presented and in public expectations had led to operational problems) and the infrastructure (a key site in a changing area).

The brief also set out to draw competitors' attention to the 'considerable amount of thought already given over the years by many excellent minds to the planning of the South Bank' and devoted a major section to an inventory of these ideas. The aim was to enable competitors to 'select and prioritise' rather than waste time reinventing what had already been proposed.

Competitors were given information on the funding stategy and asked to set out a development strategy which could accommodate this.

The two-day briefing colloquium gave competitors the opportunity to question and clarify the written brief as well as examine the existing buildings and site.

Costs and prizes

By the time the result had been announced, the exhibition mounted and the first round of consultation completed, the selection procedure had cost the South Bank Board £220 000. This included the payment of an honorarium of £10 000 to each of the ten pre-finalists plus an additional prize fund of £8000. (The money paid to the winner would be regarded as an advance of fees 'if and when engaged to carry out the work'.) It also covered fees for assessors and technical advisers and DEGW's fees for the development of the brief.

The South Bank Board received a grant of £100 000 from central government (through English Partnerships) towards the cost of organising the selection procedure and an Arts Council Architecture Award towards the cost of mounting the exhibition of shortlisted schemes.

The cost to the winning team of preparing its submission has been estimated as £100 000.

Timetable

The South Bank Board announced its intention to promote some form of competition in September 1993. The adviser, and subsequently the briefing team, were appointed soon after and the competition was officially launched at the opening of the Architecture Foundation exhibition at the beginning of February 1994. An announcement had already been circulated to the international press. Work on the brief continued until March 1994.

Closing date for 'expressions of interest'	14 March 1994
Brief sent to ten shortlisted entrants	21 March 1994
Two day briefing colloquium	14–15 April 1994
Second-stage submissions	24 June 1994
Presentations and interviews	30 June–1 July 1994
Three finalists notified	8 July 1994
Final-stage submissions	12 August 1994
Decision and assessors report by	29 August 1994
Exhibition and consultation meetings	20 September–23 October 1994

Figure 11.9 South Bank Centre proposals. Architects: Richard Rogers Partnership

Winner's approach

The Queen Elizabeth Hall, Purcell Room and part of the Hayward Gallery are covered with a canopy based on the principle of a 'crystal palace'. Extending to the riverside walk, it creates sheltered open areas for bars, restaurants, shops and performance spaces. Two new piazzas are created to the north and south sides of the Royal Festival Hall and walkways around it are removed so that circulation returns to ground level. On the riverside there is an informal piazza with a new arena for outside performances surrounded by broad curving grass terraces; beneath this arena is a new underground auditorium.

A new bridge leads from Waterloo Station concourse, across York Road and down to ground level. A wide pedestrian passerelle, with moving pavements and observation decks offering views along the Thames, replaces the Hungerford pedestrian bridge:

> The main objective was to double the number of people who visit the site by making the South Bank visible from the north bank, providing easier access, creating a comfortable environment all year round and ensuring that the area becomes both a place to see and be seen.
> The unification of the site by the act of enclosure achieves many of the desired parameters.

Promoter's response

The South Bank Board was pleased by the way the complete process went:

> It attracted a very large amount of interest, gave competitors much opportunity to understand our aspirations and requirements and particularly gave us a lot of opportunity to get to know the people we might be working with. The outcome was clear-cut and has been well received. We have had no argument or dispute as a consequence.
> Our decision to run major public exhibitions and a consultation process in parallel with the procedure was very valuable in terms of opening up the arrangements to external scrutiny . . . the final exhibition and consultation process in October 1994 provoked overwhelming endorsement for our strategy.

Outcome

The promoter plans to apply for lottery funding in order to obtain the core finance for the scheme and has already secured a grant of £1 million towards design development costs (1995). The brief required a phased solution to accommodate potential funding problems and it is likely that it will be implemented, in part, whatever the outcome of the detailed lottery application.

By going for a master plan – an approach rather than a design – the promoters have avoided criticism of details at this stage. The openness of the briefing process and the level of consultation has done much to mitigate the opposition and should help the South Bank achieve the co-operative partnership which it seeks.

Appendix RIBA project competitions 1985–1994

Year	Promoter	Project	Outcome
1985	Borough of High Peak	Sheltered housing scheme, Buxton	Project built as planned
1985	Colchester Borough Council	Council Offices	Project built as planned
1985	Chorley Borough Council (developer/architect)	Town centre private housing	Project built but with second choice of architect and different contractor
1985	Scottish Heritable Trust, York (ideas leading to a project)	Commercial riverside development	Competition winning scheme abandoned – project built using another architect
1985	Tickhill Town Council	Community Centre	Architects commissioned but project abandoned after electoral changes
1986	Aston University	Conference Centre	Project remains in development plan but no funds available to build
1986	CADW Welsh Historic Monuments	Visitor Centre at Chepstow Castle	Two different projects emerged from the competition both of which were built
1986	Bolton Metropolitan Borough Council Abbey National Building Society	Low cost housing	Project built as planned
1986	Foreign and Commonwealth Office	The British High Commissioner's New Residence, Kuala Lumpar	Project built as planned
1986	Grange School, Hartford, Cheshire	6th form accommodation	Project built as planned

Year	Promoter	Project	Outcome
1986	Royal Institute of British Architects	Architecture Centre	Abandoned through lack of funding
1986	Peterborough Methodist Circuit	New Church, Deeping St James	Project built as planned
1987	Wycombe District Council	High Wycombe Arts Centre	Competition scheme abandoned following electoral change. Alternative scheme with a different brief designed by the local authority architect
1987	Land Securities plc	Grand buildings, Trafalgar Square	Project built as planned
1987	Tewskbury Borough Council	Tewskbury Swimming Pool	Project built as planned
1988	Birmingham City Council	International competition with six small sites	No response from promoter – winners indicate limited further action
1988	Foreign and Commonwealth Office	Residence for HM Ambassador, Moscow	Situation changed and the requirement for the project disappeared
1988	Chichester District Council	Avenue de Chartres car park	Project built as planned
1989	Adur District Council	Addison Square redevelopment	Project built as planned
1989	American Plywood Association Swansea City Council	Timber framed housing	Project built as planned
1989	York City Council	Parliament Street urban design	Project built as planned

Year	Client	Project	Outcome
1990	Cardiff City Council	Cardiff Castle Visitor Centre	No further action taken
1990	Dulwich Picture Gallery Country Life Magazine (ideas leading to a project)	Extension to existing building	Fund raising project – no further action taken
1990	The Anchor Housing Association (ideas leading to a project)	Housing for the frail elderly	Original competition site lost – architects commissioned for alternative scheme
1990	The Royal National Eisteddfod of Wales	Eisteddfod Arts and Crafts Pavilion	Developed to tender stage – decision to proceed still pending
1990	The Nottingham YMCA Council	Remodelling of YMCA building	No commission – still awaiting possible funding
1991	Lancaster City Council	Morecambe seafront	No response to requests for information
1991	Property Services Agency	Inland Revenue Headquarters, Nottingham	Project built as planned
1991	The Wakefield Grammar School Foundation	School extension and private residential development on city centre site	Planning permission being sought – work scheduled for 1995 if granted
1992	The Development Board for Rural Wales	Penrhyndeudraeth Business Park in Snowdonia	Competition was for master plan – two thirds completed
1992	East Midlands Arts Board	New headquarters and gallery	Abandoned due to cost problems and reluctance to modify winning design
1993	The Richard Attenborough Centre for Disability and the Arts (see Case study 4)	New building, University of Leicester campus	Architect commissioned, project in progress
1993	The Welsh Development Agency	Pennllergaer Business Centre	Project built as planned

Year	Promoter	Project	Outcome
1993	Gateshead Metropolitan Borough Council	New housing at Windmill Hills	Subject to funding being granted
1993	South Downs Health NHS Trust (see Case study 7)	Polyclinic at Moulsecoomb, Brighton	Project built as planned
1994	University of Durham (see Case study 8)	New college	Architect commissioned, project in progress
1994	Gateshead Metropolitan Borough	Baltic Flour Mills, conversion to a visual arts centre	Subject of lottery bid
1994	South Downs Health NHS Trust (see Case study 7)	Nursing home and day care	Architect commissioned, project in progress
1994	National Glass Centre, Sunderland	Centre, workshops, factory space and visitor attractions	Subject of lottery bid
1994	Manchester City Art Gallery	Development of listed building and adjacent land	Competition in progress

Index